Walkir

By the same author

SPRINGTIME IN THE CHURCH
WE BELIEVE IN HEALING

Walking on Water

Barry Kissell

HODDER AND STOUGHTON
LONDON SYDNEY AUCKLAND TORONTO

British Library Cataloguing in Publication Data

Kissell, Barry
  Walking on water.
  1. Spiritual life
  I. Title
  269   BV4501.2

ISBN 0 340 40561 9

To Jonathan, Timothy and Noonie

Thank you for helping to hold the fort.

Acknowledgments

My special gratitude goes to David Pytches, my friend and colleague, whose unconditional love and sense of humour has made this story such fun!

To the folk at St Andrew's Chorleywood, without whose love, commitment and encouragement there would be no story to tell.

I wish to thank my secretary, Julie Evans, for her helpful comments and patience in deciphering my writing.

Contents

Foreword

Barry Kissell is a New Zealander married to an English wife, Mary. They have a family of two sons and one daughter. He has spent over twenty years of his life in the ordained ministry of the Church of England. For the last twelve years he has been Director of Faith Sharing based on St Andrew's Church, Chorleywood (Herts) – a ministry which has taken him all over the British Isles and to many countries abroad.

I first met the Kissells when I took a team to St Andrew's Church for a weekend of power evangelism in 1981 at the invitation of the vicar, David Pytches. In this book Barry tells of some of the impact our visit had on that church then, and also on the Faith Sharing teams – each team member now equipped to minister in the power of the Holy Spirit.

The book also tells of Barry's search for fulfilment in his own life, and the ministry he has exercised for the Lord. His style is gentle and his story disarming in the degree of self-disclosure. The lesson here is that God is using the walking wounded to do his work wherever they are open to the Holy Spirit and willing to step out in faith.

Barry also describes many power encounters and healings which I believe could be illuminating and inspiring for the Church of today. I am delighted to commend Barry's book.

John Wimber
Yorba Linda, California
April, 1986

Chapter 1

BEGINNINGS

Graham and I followed the metal road as it clung to the contours of the Wanganui River. South of Pipariki we parked the vehicle and started the long arduous climb into the foothills. For an hour or more we clambered along the bed of a stream before working our way to the summit.

We rested on a crag above a plateau. On the edge of the bush the deer grazed in the early morning. Our climb had started in darkness and now a gentle blue light was beginning to cast its rays upon the near end of the plateau. Our clothes were wet with perspiration and our hunting rifles weighed heavily on our shoulders.

Far below on our right, like an eel, curved the river. Above and beyond it, on the far side, a series of ranges stretched like rolling waves to snow-capped mountain peaks. Mists hung in the valleys. To our left smaller foothills eventually gave way to a horizon formed by the Tasman Sea. Dominating the skyline and appearing to rise from the ocean was the cone-shaped Mount Taranaki. It made me think of God.

I had always believed in God. Many times as a fearful child I had pulled the bedclothes over my head and asked His help. Through my turbulent teenage years I had appealed to Him in times of trouble or danger. However, I had never had an awareness of His presence.

This morning was different. Graham and I moved away from each other and sat quietly. Nothing stirred in the bush. The stillness and the beauty penetrated my heart and for the first time I was aware of God as a living presence.

The fleeting moment passed, and within an hour we had shot a young fallow deer and started our difficult descent with it to the van. Returning home, I became absorbed with my work as a trainee stock-agent auctioneer. However, I found myself reflecting more and more on my experience in the mountains, and often I would climb alone and try to recapture that moment of awareness. Mostly my sojourns in the hills proved to be times of quiet reflection, but once I again experienced what I understood to be the presence of God. Instinctively, I raised both hands into the air and walked around a hill top praising Him. I knew there was a reality which I could neither see nor touch, a reality which had no form, but whose invisible presence drew from my heart a response of praise and joy.

Near where I was lodging there were a number of churches and periodically I would attend, hoping that someone would tell me what God was like and how I could know Him. Unfortunately, this didn't happen. However, a young man who worked in a general store in our town invited me to join a party he had organised to hear Dr Billy Graham.

Athletic Park in Wellington was famous in New Zealand as a rugby stadium, and it was there that I heard a talk that was to set my life on a radically different course. Dr Graham spoke simply and sincerely. There were many quotes from the Bible interspersed with illustrations.

'If you want to know what God is like, look at Jesus Christ.' Dr Graham's voice echoed round the stadium. 'God is love, and that is what Jesus' life reflects. He loved the decaying leper, the blind, those racked with pain, the social outcasts, the prostitutes. From the cross he extended his love to a dying thief.'

Jesus' whole life was one of forgiveness said Dr Graham. The fiery Peter wanted to know how many times he had to forgive. Jesus taught that there was no limit. He demonstrated that he had authority on earth to forgive men their sins. Four men brought a friend to him on a stretcher. This man was paralysed and Jesus told him that his sins were forgiven.

'If you don't know God in a personal way it's because you are separated from him. The reason you are separated is because of your sin.' Separated by sin! I was separated. My sins were numerous. I wanted to receive the love and forgiveness of God. I wanted to know Him.

'Jesus died upon the cross to take your sins away.' The preacher stood with his hands outstretched, illustrating the position of crucifixion. He stopped speaking; there was silence. Then he repeated words of Jesus, 'My God, my God, why have you forsaken me?' (Matt. 27:46). Why did God forsake His Son? Sin separates men from God, but Jesus had never sinned. He was perfect. Then whose sin was it? It was mine.

The sermon finished, and Billy Graham was praying. I acknowledged the sin in my life, and by faith asked Jesus to live within me. I felt as if a great weight was being lifted from me. I was experiencing forgiveness, and finding that God loved me.

Enquirers were invited to gather on the rugby pitch. As I began to walk forward I heard the God of my mountain experience, the God and Father of the Lord Jesus Christ. 'What you have received, you are to share,' a voice whispered. My search had ended in, of all places, the mecca of New Zealand rugby football. Here I discovered Jesus to be the Son of God. Here I received the call to share Jesus.

I tried, when opportunities presented themselves, to share Christ, and I began to feel the call of God to leave my job at Dalgety's and become a preacher. Whenever I contemplated this, thoughts of England filled my mind, although I was a New Zealander, and loved my country. One Saturday afternoon I was at the home of my friend Dennis Wackrow. He lay on his bed, and I sat on a chair listening to records. Nearby he had a globe of the world. I began to spin it; continents and islands flashed by.

'Dennis,' I said, 'let's hitch-hike to England.' In this way, on the spur of the moment, I put into words what I believed the Lord was telling me to do.

On Monday I handed in my notice – the manager thought

I was crazy! – and Dennis took a year's leave of absence from the timber company where he was employed. We said goodbye to our colleagues, and set off. But we nearly did not leave New Zealand. On the morning of the embarkation I telephoned the shipping office to check the time of departure. The clerk said 6.00 p.m. instead of 4.00 p.m. Fortunately, we went to look over the ship at 3.55 p.m. and arrived just in time to scramble up the gangplank as it was about to be pulled up.

The great ropes which held the ship to the wharf were raised. A tug guided us into the shipping lane. Our friends on the wharf became spots of colour in the distance. The throb of the engines replaced the noises of the city. 'Farewell – land of the long white cloud.' As the shores faded, the ship began to ride the swells of the Pacific Ocean. I stood on the upper deck and the sea breeze brought back memories of surfing and freedom. Was I being impetuous? Was the Lord really calling me to England?

Rounding Cape Farewell we headed across the Tasman Sea. The sea was a monster tossing and turning; the sight of Sydney Harbour bridge was welcome indeed. This great iron expanse formed the eastern doorway to the Australian continent. We changed ships. Melbourne and Perth followed in quick succession; then we crossed the Indian Ocean to the little island of Sri Lanka.

Often at night I climbed to the upper decks to be confronted with the power, majesty and moodiness of the sea. How this contrasted with the stillness of the universe which stretched above. At such times I knew a very real communication between my spirit and the Lord. He spoke peace to my soul, reassuring me that I was on course.

We disembarked at Port Said in Egypt. Our intention was to make our way to Jerusalem, and from there hitch-hike overland to England, a journey which was still possible in the early sixties. It was winter when we arrived in the Holy City. My father was employed by UNESCO and my parents had made their home on Mount Scopus. Before leaving New Zealand we had not thought about the weather conditions in the northern hemisphere. We soon realised that it would be impossible to sleep rough during the winter months and we were glad of a family base.

We had three months to wait until the snows melted in the Lebanese mountains. We walked the places where Christ walked, and studied the incidents in the Scriptures. Days on end we sat in the souks, with the Arab merchants, watching the world go by. Christmas came and we went to Bethlehem, the focus of the thoughts of countless millions of Christians. Yet even in His land I was restless, yearning to be on the way to England.

When the weather became a little warmer we made preparations for the next phase of the journey. I had walked miles across the mountains in New Zealand with a rucksack, and knew how heavy it could become. I decided to take just a sleeping bag and a change of clothes. Taking leave of my parents, we walked to the old city of Jerusalem and followed the road leading down to Jericho. A large diesel lorry pulled up; an Arab's head appeared through the window. I told him we were going to England. He smiled as we clambered into the cab. This was the first of over two hundred lifts in cars, trucks, motorbikes, a horse and cart, a road grader and a river barge. We journeyed on for four months through Jordan, Syria, southern Turkey, Greece, Austria, Germany, Holland, and finally Belgium. At night our roof was the open sky, viewed from beaches, fields and out-houses. Our bathrooms were the rivers and lakes which crisscrossed the continents.

As we travelled we developed certain rules of the road. If a vehicle could only take one of us then the one who had the first lift would wait at the boundary of the town of destination for the other. Unfortunately, in Austria, this arrangement broke down. One morning we decided on the town of destination but somehow marked different towns on our respective maps. I waited anxiously for two days before travelling on, hoping to find Dennis. This proved impossible as we only planned a daily route and I didn't know where he was heading. Eventually he travelled north and toured Scandinavia before meeting me again in England.

Every New Zealander knows about the white cliffs of Dover. They have a place in our war memories and in the dreams of those who left England for a new life in Australasia. I first saw them in the light of a May evening, and was dismayed at the loneliness which began to grip my heart. I looked in my wallet – just five pounds! It was all I had in the world.

The cross-channel ferry landed at Folkestone. I felt rather conspicuous in my shorts, sandals and dilapidated pullover. The Customs Officer looked through my rucksack. He was a friendly sort. Once out of the Customs shed I walked towards the main road, talking to the Lord, telling Him of my arrival which, on reflection, He must have known about anyway.

'Lord, where am I sleeping tonight? How am I going to keep myself? Where am I going to live? What do you want me to do now I'm here?'

A car pulled up. I looked inside. It was the man in Customs uniform who had looked through my rucksack. He smiled and opened the passenger door. When I gave him an address in Hampshire, he invited me to spend the night at his house. His car swung into the driveway of a semi-detached home on the outskirts of Dover. He called his wife, telling her there was a visitor for supper, and a guest for the night. She had already cooked a meal for three. Since the morning she had known there was going to be a guest that night. Being a rationalist, she had discarded the thought, but as she went to town to buy supplies the impression continued, so she bought extra food and prepared it.

I was on the road early next morning. On the outskirts of Lymington in Hampshire, I was given a lift by a farmer. He asked me where I had hitchhiked from. I told him Jerusalem and that he was the final lift to my destination, number two hundred and ten! I think he thought I was joking. He took me to the home of family friends in Pennington.

St Mark's was the village church and the vicar, the Rev Peter Raban, gave me a hand of friendship. On my second evening there I fell in love with a girl in the choir – this was Mary who was later to become my wife.

I soon realised that my pursuit of God's call would involve equipping myself academically to enter a theological college, as well as keeping body and soul together. I reared chickens for Golden Produce, guarded a power station for Securicor, collected rubbish for the local council, and bored holes in pistons for Wellworthy Engineers. Always motivating me was the call to travel for God, wherever He might lead, and to share His gospel. What I was not clear about was how this would happen.

When I actually got to theological college, it was a frustrating experience. Having left school at sixteen, I found it difficult to settle down to a university standard syllabus. I frequently felt I was being trained for something I would never actually do. If I had really heard God at Athletic Park, then my future did not lie in the confines of a parish; I had to be an itinerant preacher. The other thing that rather bothered me was that I had never heard of an Anglican minister who was commissioned by the church to travel from place to place preaching the gospel.

While in my final year at London College of Divinity, I was introduced to the congregation of St Andrew's, Chorleywood – a church in the diocese of St Albans – and met John and Gay Perry. John was then vicar of St Andrew's. Our theological college was full of rumours about what was happening there so Mary and I decided to investigate for ourselves.

The first service we attended was particularly memorable. The church was so full we had to sit on the chancel steps. Although Anglican in structure, the service had tremendous life and vitality. Something was happening, but I was unable to pinpoint just what it was. I decided the vicar must have a strong personality!

John Perry's sermon seemed so ordinary, the exact opposite of what I had imagined. He read Acts 13:1–4, which describes the leaders of the church in Antioch, and the beginning of the first missionary journey of Barnabas and Paul. My attention had wandered, when suddenly I heard

John speak the words, 'The Holy Spirit said, "I want Paul and Barnabas set apart for the work to which I have called them."' As the words sank in, God said, 'You will serve me in this church.' I have now been associated with this church for twenty-one years.

A large group met in the vicarage each Friday evening, beginning at ten o'clock and going on often into the early hours of the morning. It was here that we encountered a new reality of God as the people sang, prayed, and shared their own experiences. Their fellowship and witness created a great hunger in our hearts for more of God.

On one such evening Edgar Trout from Plymouth visited, having been invited to minister. Edgar was a businessman whose life had been dramatically altered after the Lord had healed him of a back condition which had kept him bed-ridden and in severe pain. Edgar travelled widely, ministering to the believers from many denominations who met in vicarages, manses and private homes – indeed wherever there were people who wanted to discover more of God through the Holy Spirit.

Edgar prayed for us both to be filled with the Holy Spirit. I was longing for something dramatic to happen, but it all seemed very low key. He laid hands on my head and for some time prayed over me in tongues. It was not until the next morning that I experienced a release of the Holy Spirit and began myself to praise God in tongues. Mary entered into a similar experience at the same time.

My first curacy was served at St Martin's, Camborne, in the beautiful county of Cornwall. It was an evangelical church which was firmly committed to the 1662 prayer book. The PCC had as a policy rejected any of the new forms of worship or ministry and it became increasingly difficult for me to see how God could work in any new way that would relate to the people. After the sense of expectancy we had experienced in Chorleywood, that first year was very difficult indeed.

I once heard Graham Pulkingham who was minister of an episcopal church in Houston, Texas, compare and contrast the 'Church of the Spirit' with the 'Church of the Parish'. He described how he had experienced renewal in what was a relatively traditional episcopal church which had little intention of changing. He had issued an open invitation to anyone who would like to meet informally for fellowship, Bible study and prayer to come to a meeting in the rectory. Within a year or so this meeting became a 'Church of the Spirit'. Here people were filled with the Holy Spirit and were able to minister the gifts of the Spirit. Within this fellowship new hymns of worship were learnt and other forms of creative worship were encouraged. Initially this had little outward effect on what was happening in the church building on Sundays, but gradually there came a time when those involved in the rectory fellowship became the majority, and then the new life began to flow into the church. Obviously, though, this had not happened without many problems.

In St Martin's there were no groups meeting regularly to seek God in prayer, so we started one on a Friday evening in our home. For many months this consisted of the two of us, but as prayer was answered, others began to gather. Many were filled with the Holy Spirit and received the gift of tongues. Unfortunately none of the new life or insight was allowed into the 'Church of the Parish', but then I was only the curate, not the vicar.

I've seen many churches today in similar circumstances. Groups within parishes are coming alive in the Holy Spirit. Often the clergy have held back, and then new leaders appear whose desire for spiritual renewal creates a new congregation for the house church movement.

At the invitation of John Perry, we returned to Chorleywood to serve my second curacy. In our four years away there had been many changes. The congregation was now firmly established in a new church building. Worship was much more creative, incorporating new hymns from different sources, including *Sounds of Living Waters* from Graham Pulkingham's church in Houston. Dance and drama groups were also making their contribution. A successful parish mission had taken place, led by Canon Harry Sutton, and many people were meeting in home groups.

Once a month in the evening service there was special prayer for the sick, or any with particular needs. Such people were encouraged to receive their Communion last of all and to remain kneeling. The clergy and wardens would ask these people what they would like prayer for, then involve the congregation in the prayer. Though greatly appreciated, it was rather formal, concentrating on the office as seen in James chapter 5, rather than the ministry of the gifts of the Holy Spirit described in 1 Corinthians 12–14.

During my third year at St Andrew's, I had the opportunity to travel to a number of churches, and I usually took a small team with me. It was during this time that the Faith Sharing Ministry was born. I came to see that unless the goodness of God is given away to others, it will eventually rot and 'stink' like the manna in the wilderness when it was kept too long.

In the Gospels Jesus travelled and ministered in teams ranging from three to twelve. He also sent out His disciples two by two. A reading of the journeys of the greatest of all faith sharers, Paul of Tarsus, shows that this exceptionally gifted man was seldom alone. I discussed this concept of team ministry with the leadership of our church. They gave me an initial period of two years in which to experiment in this way. From the outset I called the ministry the 'Faith Sharing Ministry' as it became apparent to me that we could only offer to others what we had ourselves.

Initially I invited thirty people, representing a cross-section of our congregation, both in age and Christian experience, to join with me. Out of this team came a nucleus, trained for lay leadership, which has eventually enabled us to send out four different teams.

For seven years, we travelled around the British Isles to villages, towns and inner city churches. Usually we went for weekends, but increasingly for weeks. Through a worship group, dance, drama, preaching and testimony, people came to know Christ and the renewing presence of the Holy Spirit.

However, for me, it was becoming too routine and man-centred – little did I know that a crisis was looming on the horizon.

During this period, St Andrew's was going through its own crisis. As in my case, it was a crisis of power. We had all the outward signs of renewal, yet those of us at the heart of the church's life knew only too well that we were stuck. As with the church, so with the Faith Sharing Ministry, the freshness and spontaneity had been fossilised.

In 1977, when John Perry left to become the Warden of Lee Abbey, David Pytches came to be our vicar. David and his wife, Mary, had been missionaries with SAMS in Chile for seventeen years and during the latter part of his stay David had been appointed bishop, taking over the Diocese of Chile, Bolivia and Peru in 1971.

John had left a full-time staff of four at St Andrew's and had given responsibility to dozens of lay people. As leader and pastor, he had listened to his staff and leaders, and had always sought consensus before implementing change. Our worry was about what would happen if his successor wanted to return the church to a 'one-man show'. I had seen this happen in the early days of the renewal at a church which had been in a similar situation to ourselves. The incoming vicar had felt so threatened that he had closed down all the meetings he himself was unable to attend or lead. We subsequently led a week's mission at that church and were privileged to see it once again begin to catch the wind of the Spirit after fifteen years in the doldrums.

Our worries were unfounded. As soon as I met David I, with others, realised that he was God's man. On a cold winter's evening we sat together in our lounge. He said that he wanted us all to stay and saw himself fitting into the team and developing what God was already doing. As we started to get to know each other, David shared what he'd seen God doing in many of the pentecostal churches in South America. I could understand his accounts of healing as, in minor and less dynamic ways, we had experienced similar cases. People and places that were demonised were slightly out of our regular experience, as were the numerous accounts of people having their teeth filled miraculously in worship meetings. David told me he had to stop telling these stories in his missionary deputation work as it made people so angry. He had seen more of the powerful working of God than I had, and yet it was not until his friend came from America that we began to witness these things in our own ministries.

One day, when I returned with a team from a week's mission, David greeted me with the news that he had met a man who had discovered how we could minister the power of God. He was an American and David had invited him and his team to our church for the following weekend. My heart fell – we had had Americans at the church before. Some had been rather insensitive and brash and their triumphalistic approach had put many off, including myself. However, David and I always trusted and supported each other, so I refrained from comment and awaited the arrival of our visiting preacher with interest.

John Wimber, a sun-tanned, bearded, 'teddy bear' shaped character, was already at the vicarage when Mary and I arrived for supper. He was neither selling himself nor his 'product', which struck me as being rather un-American! David, in his usual enthusiastic way, had described our ministry to John and, to my embarrassment, the Faith Sharing Ministry became the main topic of conversation. John seemed genuinely interested – it was only afterwards that I realised that he was holding back a handful of aces.

We gathered together in the church for the Saturday evening meeting and John led a time of worship on the piano. He sought in a gentle, quiet way to connect our hearts with the heart of God. I was unable to verbalise what was happening, but I realised it was different from what we had experienced as a church before.

With much humour John then introduced a team he had brought with him from Los Angeles. Various members described how the power of God had come into their lives and transformed them. There were marriages that had been renewed, organic diseases healed, obsessional habits broken.

Besides that, the team seemed to be so in touch with God and yet so relaxed and open. John spoke simply about the empowering of the Holy Spirit. Unfortunately, it was at that moment that I had to leave for the airport to meet my parents who were just arriving from New Zealand.

When I returned home, it was late and yet my wife, Mary, was still at the church. To while away the time, I tuned in to a late night film on ITV. I was well into the film when she came into the lounge. She looked quite different and asked me if I minded if she just sat quietly by herself on the sofa. She sat with her eyes closed and her hands before her in an open position. By nature she is a great talker, but here she was asking whether we could just sit in quietness together! Obligingly, I turned off the television and sat with her into the early hours.

Eventually we went to bed. I have never felt such peace and power emanating from a person before, not to mention the heat! Lying beside her in bed was like having my back to a roaring fire in the midst of winter. Most of my night was spent with the duvet off and one leg resting on the ground! I was longing to hear what had actually happened in the church after I had left.

Mary told me the next morning that, after John had finished speaking, he welcomed the Holy Spirit to come and minister the life of Jesus to the people. Initially it was all quiet and many felt embarrassed, but then all sorts of things began to happen to people. In the midst of all this, John said that God was anointing people for a healing ministry and the sign was that their hands were hot and tingling. It was at that moment that Mary felt something like a powerful electric current running through her hands. She went to the front with the rest and was anointed with oil whereupon the fire of God swept through her whole body; this was the anointing that burned in her all night.

It was with a certain amount of apprehension that I looked forward to Sunday. In the morning John spoke on 'Glossolalia'; it was a disaster. This was his first sermon in an Anglican liturgical service and he seemed to be reading from lecture notes. He used theological terms and spoke of the early Church Fathers with such a pronounced Californian brogue that most of the congregation had little or no idea what he was talking about. He seemed far too academic for us and his accent was too unfamiliar. However, the evening was dramatically different.

We had a short evening service; then opportunity was given for those who wished to leave during the last hymn. The church was packed, and except for a few who had to relieve baby sitters, all stayed. John then briefly introduced Lonnie Frisby to us. What he said about him meant nothing to us, except that, like Arthur Blessit, he was one of the hippie evangelists used in the Californian revival in the early sixties.

Our neighbours, the Roberts, had had Lonnie and a friend with them for the day. Lonnie had spent most of the morning pacing silently and uncommunicatingly round the house, and after Sunday lunch had asked for a blanket in which he proceeded to wrap himself in and then lie on the floor of their living room, sleeping in a foetal position until just before the evening service. We did not know if this was jet lag or Jesus people ritual.

As Lonnie stood up to speak that night I remembered Iain's description of his Sunday. However, the talk he gave us was biblical, simple and delivered with intense conviction. Nothing new, I thought. In a less dramatic way I had sought to convey the same truth many times. Suddenly he stopped as if in mid-flight. He then announced that God was going to confirm the truth of his message with signs and wonders. I had hoped this would happen, yet in my heart I was saying, 'Oh, yeah?'

I was at the front, behind the Communion table which commanded a perfect view of the proceedings. Lonnie asked the congregation to stand. He said the Holy Spirit was coming upon people at the right hand corner of the church at the back. I looked to see what he was seeing, and suddenly a number of people collapsed on the floor. He then announced that the Holy Spirit was falling upon the second row of the right hand side – a row of young people went down like a pack of cards.

Mike, a young man who was to become David's son-in-law, was leaning against the wall, surveying the scene cynically. Lonnie asked him what he thought and he replied that it was all emotional. Lonnie proceeded to tell him that what he was seeing was the power of God and asked him if he wanted any further assurance on the subject. He said he did, and so Lonnie joined his hand to one of the young people swaying under the power of the Holy Spirit. Immediately the power of God flowed into Mike and he became a believer. Within days he had offered his help in the Sunday School.

Many people in the church were in tears; a number who had experienced physical healing were either sitting filled with wonder or sharing what had happened with anyone who would listen. Others were lost in worship, adoration and thanksgiving. Many were speaking in tongues for the first time. I realised that this was the missing dimension – here was power.

John Wimber's team began to walk amongst our congregation, praying gently for people upon whom the Spirit was coming. I didn't quite know what to do, so sat quietly and opened my heart afresh to Jesus, asking for power so that I myself could be effective in ministering to people's real needs. I had my eyes closed and sensed someone was standing in front of me. It was Lonnie. He said that the Spirit of God was coming upon me like a mighty wind. As he spoke I felt, as I often used to whilst walking alone on empty Cornish beaches in late autumn, a wind blowing on my face, ruffling my hair. Deep within I knew that this was it – I was in touch with the power of God.

As I returned home that evening many thoughts crowded my mind. I wondered how we could introduce what we had seen and experienced into our regular church life and, ultimately, into the Faith Sharing Ministry. What would people think? Would God work in the same way through our ministry? What if we invited the Holy Spirit to minister and nothing happened? Would other churches be prepared to welcome this new emphasis?

Whatever happened I knew I was unable to deny this new work of God. I realised that it would mean allowing God to be God. This would involve giving Him the opportunity of speaking and acting. From now on it would be different, but how different I could never have visualised.

Chapter 2

BY WORD AND DEED

Evangelicals are great expounders and explainers. I had not been brought up in that tradition – in fact, after my conversion I joined a middle-of-the-road Anglican church with its ten-minutes-a-week 'sermonette', in the context of the weekly parish eucharist and Sunday afternoon Bible study run by a committed lay member.

My first contact with evangelicals was at my theological college. I had been recommended to that particular college by Canon Busby, the Director of Ordinands for the Winchester diocese. When I applied to be considered for the Anglican ministry, I was referred to him. In his gentle, gracious way he welcomed me to his study and invited me to tell my story. I mentioned that I had come to know Christ at a Billy Graham meeting. 'Ah,' he said, 'you must be an evangelical.' Well, fancy that, I thought – I must be an evangelical – what a long word!

I well remember being summoned into the study of a fellow student who was in his last year of training at that college. Sitting behind his large oak desk, which he had imported from the bank, he announced that my fellow students were rather worried about me. In his words, I was 'losing my cutting edge'. It transpired that I had been observed going down to the 'local' with another student who, in their eyes, was 'beyond the pale'. From an early age, as a trainee auctioneer in New Zealand, I had always been accustomed to entertain clients at the 'local' after the stock

sales. I couldn't quite understand the difficulty my fellow
students were having.

I found a common bond with evangelicals in their love for
Scripture. It has been my discipline and delight for nearly
twenty years to read the Scriptures daily and meditate upon
the truths which they contain. However, I found that within
this tradition there was little room for a sense of mystery. Yet
Paul, for all his intellectual brilliance, retained a sense of awe
and wonder, and could say of God '. . . who lives in un-
approachable light, whom no one has seen or can see' (1
Tim. 6:16).

A mystery, by definition, is not something that can be fully
understood. Speaking in tongues is part of the mystery; Paul
instructs the Corinthians that those who speak in tongues
speak not to man but to God because they utter mysteries in
the Spirit (1 Cor. 14:2). The human intellect is limited;
although much can be understood, the mind, vast areas of
the supernatural are beyond human reason and belong to the
area of mystery.

During the early sixties God poured out His Spirit in a new
way and what is now known as 'the charismatic movement'
came into being. In the Anglican Church the main group
of people at first involved were the evangelicals, Michael
Harper, a curate at All Souls, Langham Place, being one of
them. This was a matter of great concern. The majority of
evangelicals were 'cessationists'; they taught that the ministries and gifts of the Holy Spirit had ceased with the writing
of the New Testament and the death of the apostles. Some
said publicly that speaking in tongues and other manifestations of the Holy Spirit were devilish in origin. Others
maintained that this was from God and cited the Acts of the
Apostles as authenticating the present movement.

There was much to rejoice about in the charismatic renewal. Countless thousands of lives were touched in new
ways by the Spirit of God. Most English Christians still seem
to live under the Law and have great difficulty with the
freedom of the Spirit or in believing that God really loves and
accepts them. We live in what must be one of the most

negative and critical cultures in the world. I well remember writing to a feature writer of a daily national newspaper, commending him on an article in which I thought he had given a fair assessment of a Christian situation. My letter comprised one short paragraph. He wrote back a full typed page telling me about his work and family. In the hyper-critical atmosphere of Fleet Street that was probably the only encouraging letter he had ever received.

Through the charismatic renewal Christians were freed from the 'ought' of the law, and were entering into a new relationship with Jesus based on love. As a result they began to worship God in a way never dreamed of before. For many the prayer gift of tongues became a feature. Some felt that at last they had a faith worth sharing and in informal situations talked about Christ with neighbours and work colleagues. A concern for the social needs of the area developed in practical ways.

But the movement also had its limitations. The evangelicals above all love the preacher and teacher. At conferences we sat for hours as biblical teachers 'opened' the Scriptures. Around these highly gifted Bible expositors devoted followers gathered. The teacher's particular way of interpreting the Scriptures becomes the touchstone of orthodoxy. And charismatics, who taught endlessly about the every-member-body-ministry, very quickly produced their own 'gurus'. For years at all the major conferences the same names appeared on the brochures – they still do today. Their publications heralded the end of the one man ministry and yet they were so conditioned by their past that, with a few exceptions, the body ministry was little in evidence.

As with the leadership, so with the gifts of the Spirit: the evangelical charismatics applied the same cultural yardsticks. Its leaders sought to explain and expound it – we had international, national and local conferences on the ministry and gifts of the Holy Spirit. Modern authors expounded and explained in minute detail the various aspects of the Holy Spirit's ministry.

We at St Andrew's were no different. Even now I have files

of notes on the courses we taught during that period. In minute detail we covered every aspect of the Spirit's work in the individual and the church. We taught what the Scriptures said. Our conviction was that God had never changed and what He did at the beginning He could do today. Many in the congregation had experienced a new working of the Holy Spirit within their lives and in private quite a large proportion used the gift of tongues. Once a month we had prayer for healing at our evening Communion Service, but with rare exceptions there was little physical healing and those who testified to how the Lord had healed them spoke of inner hurts and psychological problems. Whilst gathering material for the book *Springtime in the Church* I had great difficulty in finding people to interview who had actually been healed physically. For all our teaching on prophecy, little was experienced even at the informal mid-week meeting and none in the Sunday services.

We were once asked by the Faith and Order Committee of the Church of England to put on an evening which members of the General Synod would be invited to attend. The idea was that, with a team, we would explain the ways in which the charismatic renewal had influenced our church and parish. Armed with an overhead projector, a worship group and dancers, we made our way to the planned rendezvous. To my surprise the hall adjacent to the General Synod was relatively full. Amongst the 170 there was almost an equal division between clerics and laity. In our preparation we had listed areas which had been influenced by the renewal. Members of our team spoke of new forms of worship, of how fellowship groups had been formed, of our new approach to finance, of the beginnings of the Healing Ministry, of the concern for evangelism within the parish, and the ministry of the Faith Sharing teams.

In order that the presentation should not be just an exchange of facts, we led a worship time and our dancers danced. I went home depressed and downcast. There had been no revelations, no prophecy, no tongues or interpretation. Those who had brought their problems with them returned home with the same problems. For all our teaching on the healing ministry, the sick had not been healed. We were a classic case of the expounders and explainers. When John Wimber and his team visited us they helped us to see how we could stand back and allow the Holy Spirit complete freedom to work in power in whatever way He wished.

I have often tried to put myself in the shoes of Elisha after his mentor, Elijah, had been taken to heaven in the fiery chariot. He had watched dumbfounded as Elijah had raised the dead, healed the lepers, called upon God to burn up the altar he had soaked with water. Then Elijah told his disciple that he was leaving him. Elisha would soon have to see if the God of Elijah would be active also with him. After John Wimber left, David had to see if God would be active in the same way through him also.

Following John Wimber's visit church members began to pray for each other in a new way. In the past, the leaders would ask those seeking help what they would like prayer for. We would then lay hands on them and pray accordingly. Now those praying for others would simply ask the Holy Spirit to come upon the person requesting prayer. We would then encourage the person in need also to welcome the Holy Spirit.

Jesus said that He only spoke what He heard from the Father and only did what He saw the Father doing (John 5:19; 8:26). When Jesus went to Bethesda, the local 'hospital' in Jerusalem (the equivalent to Bath Spa), He saw a crowd of disabled folk jostling each other for prime positions near the pool. One man there had been crippled from birth. For thirty years he had been completely dependent upon the care and thoughtfulness of others. Jesus perceived that the Father now wanted to heal him and so Jesus told him to pick up his mat and walk.

John the Baptist saw the Holy Spirit coming on Jesus at His baptism. The Father had told John that he would know the Messiah through observing the coming of the Holy Spirit on Him (John 1:32–34). This may have been one of the ways Jesus discerned who the Father wanted to heal.

I have found that there are a number of symbols which seem to relate in a special way to healing. I rise at 6.00 a.m. most mornings and on one particular day I awoke just before the alarm shattered the stillness. Into my mind came the words, 'Fire, wind, oil and water are not just symbols of My Spirit – they describe the action of My Spirit.' I felt that God was telling me something important. The words were so clear that I jumped out of bed and ran downstairs to my study where I wrote them out before I could forget them.

This made sense to me. In my experience these words describe accurately what can happen to people when the Holy Spirit comes upon them for blessing. My friend Charles Whitehouse invited me to speak at a series of meetings he was holding in a school hall. Charles was appointed by Cardinal Hume to be the lay leader of the Renewal Movement within the Roman Catholic Church. On the evening in question about 150 attended and after I had spoken we had a time of prayer for those in need.

Mary and I had just finished praying for a lady when we both sensed the presence of a wind within the hall. All the curtains started to billow and a hatch leading to a kitchen rattled. This lasted for about ten seconds. Simultaneously we realised that it was the presence of the Holy Spirit. On checking afterwards, all the windows and doors were fastened tightly as it was a cold November evening.

On another occasion we were with a team at Corwen in Wales. It was a balmy summer evening and after the vicar, Meirion Griffiths, had welcomed us, he apologised to the crowd for the lack of ventilation. He explained that the windows in the hall were permanently locked. At the prayer time I felt a cool wind blowing over me. It started on my hands and eventually moved to my chest and face. I could see that other people were being affected in the same way and I invited them to gather at the front. They stood and the wind intensified upon them as they were caught up in the worship of God.

In the situations I have described not everybody was aware of the wind of the Spirit. This was equally true of our team. It transpired that only half were aware of what was happening. However, since these instances, I find that it is now commonplace for people at our meetings to experience the Holy Spirit as I have described.

I was once a speaker in a series of meetings on healing which some Roman Catholic priests had arranged for churches in the Woking area. A Baptist minister and I had prayed for a lady in a wheelchair. After a period of waiting on the Lord, I asked her if she felt anything. She indicated that her shoulder had become progressively warmer and at that moment was particularly hot. I looked at her shoulder and saw that my colleague was holding his hand about six inches away from it. I moved my hand between his and the lady's shoulder and felt a powerful energy flowing out of his hand. Conscious that it was her back that needed healing, I suggested that he place his hand there. Immediately she testified to a warmth flowing down her back.

When we prayed for people in our church, we would ask them to describe what was happening. Sometimes they reported nothing, but in a healing context people often described feelings of fire or heat in the damaged area. Again, others would say that they felt as if a warm oil was flowing through their mind, bringing a sense of deep peace.

It was said of Moses that after he had been up into the mountain to be with God, his face shone. In fact it shone so much that he had to cover it when returning to the camp because the people were unable to look at him. I noticed that when the Holy Spirit came upon a person, there was often a sheen upon the face and at times this could be quite bright. The person concerned would afterwards testify to being full of the presence and peace of the Lord.

Sometimes people would shake violently, or for a period of time breathe deeply. We noticed also that as the Holy Spirit began his ministry people's eyelashes would start to flutter at an extraordinary rate. Sometimes there was holy laughter and sometimes there were tears. Some would just kneel and weep, silently, while others cried with deep groans of agony and pain. We had to place packets of tissues by the

Communion table as often people came quite unprepared and had nothing with which to mop away their tears.

One particular phenomenon slightly troubled me. At times people would just collapse and lie full length on the sanctuary floor. They seemed to have a range of experiences. Some felt a quiet peace which could last for an hour or more, while others writhed and twisted about in apparent agitation. I had initially seen this on television and had been quite put off. Those who wanted prayer had stood in a line before the camera. The preacher walked by, placing hands on their heads. Immediately they would fall backwards into the hands of a 'catcher'. It seemed to me to be a prime example of auto-suggestion in an emotionally charged atmosphere.

The first experience of this in my own ministry happened in Canada. I was speaking at a lunchtime meeting in a little church on the outskirts of Toronto. Having concluded my address, I invited people to come forward for prayer. The first was a middle-aged lady of extremely large proportions. She was followed by a younger man, thin and bespectacled, about five feet tall. She stood in front of the Communion rail and I was just about to place my hand on her head when she collapsed like a deflated air balloon, right on to the little man who had been standing close behind her. She had become a dead weight and it was with some difficulty that we extracted him from under her!

Since that time this phenomenon has become a more regular occurrence. Sometimes it happens in the worship and the congregation may hear a slight thump as a worshipper falls back into his seat to rest in the Spirit. However, it happens most frequently as people are praying for others. During those times a deep inner healing is often taking place. With the continual breakdown of family life and the decadence within our society, more people than ever are suffering from invisible traumas which cripple their emotions. It would seem to me that the Lord takes away consciousness in order to begin to heal some of those deep and crippling hurts.

As those who are praying for the sick wait upon the Holy

Spirit, He may manifest His presence in some of the ways already described. When this happens, those involved can just bless what God is doing. On other occasions the Lord reveals what He is doing through a word of knowledge. This may come to one or more of those praying. Often this word reveals the sources of the illness or problem. A lady wanting prayer for an irrational fear which had tormented her for most of her life came to the rail for help. Patsy and Mary were praying with her, and Patsy had a word of knowledge regarding a bicycle. Mary asked if this meant anything to her. It transpired that as a child of five the lady had suffered a traumatic accident when she had lost control of her bicycle while riding down a hill. The team then prayed about this event and she became free from that particular fear. Prior to the prayer of blessing at the end of our services David asks the congregation to be still. He then invites the Holy Spirit to release His gifts upon the people. At this point some are given words of knowledge, and those to whom the words apply are invited forward for prayer. Those who have been authorised to pray for healing then form groups of two or three and begin to pray for them. I have often had a picture of Jesus attending a typical Anglican service of worship. He sits in the middle of the church, not at the back as He is not 'Church of England'. The opening hymn is announced, the choir processes in and is installed by the final verse. Then the liturgy starts – confession . . . absolution . . . readings are followed by canticles. Jesus is watching and wondering whether He may have an opportunity to do something before the set prayers. Alas, no, for we are now into the notices. Then comes the hymn (during which the offerings must be taken), then the sermon. After the sermon would be a good opportunity He thinks, but a hymn and blessing follow, after which the choir moves out, singing a recessional. Within ten minutes the building is empty. The congregation had assembled with all its problems, only to take them home again, and will return with them once more the following week. Jesus had longed to be able to meet with them and minister to them through the Body but, alas, there was little opportunity.

Ministering in the way I have described gives opportunities to touch people at their points of need. We find that the problem presented is not necessarily the real problem. Peter knelt at the Communion rail and before we engaged him in conversation he blurted out that he wanted God to heal a pain in his neck which had troubled him for many years. Welcoming the Holy Spirit, we waited, praying silently in tongues. Through a word of knowledge it was revealed that he suffered from a deep anxiety whose roots went back over many years. As prayer was made for this, there was an immediate releasing and freeing from the neck pain.

Obviously such a ministry has some inherent problems. One is that those anointed for healing can become an elitist group and this undermines the concept of an every man ministry. Starting a healing ministry at all can be divisive. It is quite extraordinary how threatening this is to some people.

David started periodic Saturday morning talk-backs. The policy has always been to keep these meetings open so that everyone who wants to voice an opinion can do so. There were a number of medical doctors and others in the congregation who had difficulties ranging from questions about doctrine and practice to decency and order in the prayer time after the services.

Today, five years later, I perceive that this was one of the key elements in the harmonious development of the healing ministry. Obviously we did not always agree with each other, and the initial meetings were sometimes quite confrontational. However, instead of sharing our disapproval in little groups which might foster dissension, we learned to listen to each other. Although the leadership had no intention of retreating from what we felt the Lord was showing us, we tried to listen with great care to the critics, and where it was possible to accommodate, we did.

Michael Green, my New Testament tutor at theological college, used to say that reading or hearing Paul's epistles was like listening to one participant in a telephone conversation. The apostle was answering questions that perplexed the New Testament church, and his replies were based on his understanding of the Scriptures and the Christian teaching passed to him and on his experiences of the living Christ and the workings of His Spirit. A theologian who wishes to speak with any relevance should be a person who lives in a Spirit-filled community and brings a biblical understanding to the experiences of the Holy Spirit which are common to that community. That is what we as leaders tried to do.

After three months the Saturday morning talk-backs ceased and were replaced by teaching sessions for those who were involved in the healing ministry. David sought to provide scriptural principles and practical teaching to undergird the developing ministry. From this material came his book *Come, Holy Spirit.**

This initial group has continued to expand so that now some 120 people are authorised to be involved in the ministry of healing at the rails. One primary qualification is that these people should be in the process of being healed themselves as they are open to the Holy Spirit's on-going work in their own lives. We are very much 'the walking wounded' as we minister to others. Only when we get to heaven will the work of wholeness be complete. Until then the Holy Spirit will be continually seeking to fashion us into a likeness of Jesus. Besides physical healing, this will involve, amongst other things, the healing of our emotional lives as well as the renewal of our minds and freedom from the power of sin. What we find increasingly is that at one time we will be praying for others, and at other times they will be praying for us. In this ministry there is no place for people who are above being ministered to themselves.

They should also have received an anointing from God for the work of healing. Often the Holy Spirit will come upon their hands, bringing the sensation of tingling or the pulsations of an electric current. Whenever I became aware that this was happening, I would invite those having that experience to come forward where we could pray for them. It has been my custom to anoint their hands with oil and to bless

* *Come, Holy Spirit* by David Pytches (Hodder & Stoughton, 1985).

what the Holy Spirit has been doing within them. As we do this it is not uncommon for the anointing of the Spirit to increase on them.

It is said of Jesus that He was moved with compassion when He saw the crowds because they appeared to Him to be like sheep without a shepherd. Compassion must be a characteristic of any person seeking to minister healing. It is often through intense feelings of compassion that a person is called into the healing ministry. I have also seen large numbers of people who have not received an obvious and dramatic anointing but whose hearts have been so full of compassion that they have wept as they ministered healing to others.

In his teaching David would often say that we were not offering people a counselling ministry when they came forward for prayer. If people needed counselling, then they could make an appointment with a pastoral counsellor. We were simply offering a ministry of the Holy Spirit. We were taught how to welcome the Holy Spirit upon a person and shown the ways in which we could know His presence. We were a church which for years had held seminars and series on the gifts of the Holy Spirit. We were great expounders and explainers. Now we were actually learning to minister in the gifts of the Holy Spirit. We had begun to do the work.

Chapter 3

GIFTS FROM GOD

One Sunday we were commissioned by the church in preparation for taking a team on a six week overseas tour. Afterwards I went to the door to speak with people as they left. Olive took me aside and told me she had a message from God for me. Slightly taken aback, I listened as she related how the previous evening God told her that on the aeroplane I would meet and talk with a certain man. Our conversation would be meaningful to him, but I was not to be taken aback by his response.

In the feverish activity which surrounds such a trip this conversation was soon forgotten. Eventually our flight took us over northern Australia and as the sky was clear I went to a window at the back of the jumbo to have an uninterrupted view of the land. I was leaning against the emergency door, looking through the window, when I was joined by a man. Suddenly the conversation with Olive came rushing back into my mind. The Lord seemed to be saying that this was the man I had been told about.

We started to talk. He was an Australian and he told me that he had been a Methodist minister responsible for a number of apparently successful churches. Five years previously he had had a crisis of faith. His problem was that he had never seen God in action in his ministry or churches and had become disillusioned with the New Testament. He had left the ministry and was now in business.

I listened to him for twenty minutes before he asked me

what I did. In my reply I was able to share a number of instances when we had seen God doing today exactly what he had done in the New Testament. My heart went out to this man and I wanted to pray with him for the filling of the Holy Spirit. However, he ended the conversation abruptly and returned to his wife – just as the word of knowledge said he would.

God is all-knowing about every person. Psalm 139 tells us that He knows our moment-by-moment posture – whether we are standing up or sitting down. He knows every thought that goes through our mind. Our first conscious memories, whether in the womb or the outside world, are known to Him.

It would appear that the Holy Spirit imparts a fragment of this information through a 'word of knowledge' in order that God can make His purpose known. He wanted me to know about the meeting in the jumbo so that when it happened I would not be taken aback by the reactions. Jesus wanted to introduce the woman at the well in Samaria to a quality of life that had always eluded her. She had many barriers but the breakthrough came when He told her to fetch her husband. In her reply she made out that she was single. It seems probable that Jesus ministered to her through a 'word of knowledge'. He told her that she had had five husbands and the man she was living with at that moment was not her husband. It would appear from the story that Jesus revealed to her much more about her life than recorded by John because in the village afterwards she invited people to 'come see a man who told me everything that I have ever done'.

This gift is used by God, as the above instance illustrates, to stop a person in his tracks, causing him to review his life as it relates to God. Some winters ago Mary and I were having a few days' break in the New Forest. One cold evening we went to a pub called 'The Red Lion' where we planned to sit and talk before a roaring log fire. As I was buying the drinks I saw a couple sitting behind a table at the fireside. She was probably in her early twenties and he in his mid-forties. They were obviously very fond of each other and I wondered how they had come to be together.

As I left the bar he smiled and invited us to sit with them. The young lady was an Australian and we talked about places we knew in common. He asked me what I did. I was just about to answer him when the Holy Spirit told me that he was a priest. I said simply that I was like him – a priest. He was too – I was Anglican and he was a Roman Catholic priest. His expression was one of incredulity. Where had we met before? Had I been to Rome? No! Had we met in some city in Australia? Had I seen him on the television? No! No! It sounded presumptuous to say that God had told me about him.

Through this 'word of knowledge' they were enabled, like the woman of Samaria, to begin to face up to the difficult situation they had got themselves into. God was just letting them know He knew all about them and wanted to help them.

Much of our outreach in the Faith Sharing Ministry is based on people's homes. Here the host and hostess will invite their friends to meet us and share in a discussion on the relevance of the Christian faith. On one such occasion we were leading a week in the north of England. The meeting, which a colleague and I had been leading, had reached an apparent impasse. A young couple, who had spent nearly all the evening questioning quite aggressively, had ended up by dismissing our claims concerning Jesus Christ. The wife had said she was unable to believe. Just at that moment the Holy Spirit told me that the problem was her involvement in occult practices. As I said this, other insights were given and within moments she was asking what she could do to know Christ. Later that evening she knelt on the kitchen floor, repented of her sins, renounced all evil, and received Christ. Her husband joined with her.

It is well known that traumas experienced in childhood – or even in the womb – can beset a person all through life, often leading to irrational fears and behaviour. Sometimes, however, knowledge of these traumas eludes the most skilled of counsellors; and even when they are discerned the wisdom to know how to deal with them may be lacking.

Jean was in her early thirties, married and with a young family. She was constantly overwhelmed by feelings of fear which made her panic and weep in despair. As we prayed with her, the Holy Spirit showed me a picture of a girl of eight standing on a high wall by the sea. Suddenly I saw her falling and half way down her foot was caught in a protruding branch. I saw a terrified little girl hanging, head downwards, many feet above the beach. When I told her what I felt the Holy Spirit was showing me, she said that this was an exact description of a childhood experience which had implanted a deep fear in her heart.

Paul reminded the young Timothy that the Spirit God gives is not one of fear but of love, power, and of sound mind (see 2 Tim. 1:7). In Romans 5:5 he maintained that the love of God is poured into the human heart by the Holy Spirit. In Jesus' name we welcomed the Holy Spirit into Jean's life and a wonderful healing took place as love displaced fear.

Often the Holy Spirit gives those receiving the 'word of knowledge' brief symptoms of the disease or damage which He wants to heal. During the worship time at one of our Saturday Celebration meetings I began to sense an increasing heat in my left ear. The heat started in the outer ear and moved to the inner. At one stage it was as much as I could bear. When the leader of the meeting called for 'words of knowledge', I indicated that I felt God wanted to heal a person with damage in his left ear. Later that evening a clergyman friend told me that he had responded to that word and been healed of deafness in his left ear. Apparently as a young man he had enjoyed twelve-bore shooting and the noise of one discharge had deafened his ear.

David often has 'words of knowledge' through this means. Recently at the end of a Communion service he momentarily felt a shooting pain in his right knee. He gave this word out just prior to the Blessing at the end of the service. At the ministry time two ladies approached me. One of them was there simply to accompany the other who, it transpired, had suffered from continuous pain in her right knee. The lady concerned came reluctantly as she was staying in the parish with her friend and had never experienced prayer for a healing ministry before. Mary and I welcomed the Holy Spirit upon her and in Jesus' name asked Him to heal her knee. She felt a gentle heat in the damaged area and then we saw her knee begin to move in different directions. Within less than a minute she said quietly that she had been healed – one of the quickest healings I have ever witnessed.

People often say to me, 'If only I had your faith.' Usually that is an excuse for not taking the claims of Jesus seriously and by an act of the will making a commitment to Him. After Sunday lunch at a vicarage on a Faith Sharing weekend a student lodging with the family asked how she could come to know Christ. During the Saturday I had talked with her at some length about Jesus. Now she wanted to know Him. I encouraged her to welcome Him into her life simply by asking. As she did this, the Holy Spirit came powerfully upon her and, although sitting, she rested in the Spirit for thirty minutes or more. It became obvious that with His coming He had started to heal some deep hurts which emanated from her childhood. This initial act of opening one's life to Christ is saving faith.

Having come to know Christ, we become pilgrims in the life of faith. Paul summarised this 'living faith' in his testimony to the Philippians when he wrote: 'The life I live in the body, I live by faith in the Son of God, who loved me and gave himself for me' (Gal. 2:20). On this pilgrimage we walk by faith and not by sight.

Richard Wood was the brother of Harding Wood, both well known and loved evangelists. It was my privilege, while a curate in Camborne, to take Communion to Richard who lived in Chasewater with his daughter and her husband. He died in his ninety-ninth year and our friendship had spanned ten years. Richard epitomised this 'living faith'. We were visiting Cornwall with a team and I took the opportunity to call on him. As it happened, it was a few months before he died. It was winter-time and we found Richard wrapped in sheepskin rugs. This little wizened old man simply glowed. His mental powers were fully intact. Bubbling with excitement and anticipation, he spoke of heaven which he had obviously glimpsed by faith. He was so looking forward to his meeting with Jesus and to being united with his wife and family. Within a short time he would have no need for faith because he was going to see the One in whom he had believed.

The gift of faith is something different again. It is that faith which moves mountains. With this gift comes an inner certainty that what God has said will eventually take place. Jesus walked down to Bethany four days after hearing the news that Lazarus was ill. He approached his friend's house knowing that Lazarus was dead but firmly believing that there was going to be a resurrection. Moses experienced the gift of faith at the Red Sea and Elijah on Mount Carmel. Peter exercised it when he walked on the water, and Paul as he was saved from a shipwreck in the stormy Aegean.

A lady had come forward for prayer at one of our morning services. In a routine way I asked her what she would like prayer for. To my consternation she requested sight in her right eye which had ceased to function. I had no doubt that Jesus could heal, but I had no faith that it would happen with her. There were four of us in the group prayer for her. To fill in the time while I worked out how we should handle the situation I said, 'Let's be still and open to the Lord.' Suddenly a young American from a team visiting the church put his hand on her eye and said with great confidence, 'In the name of Jesus, be healed.' I watched and waited. He then asked her if anything was happening in the eye. She indicated that some blurred sight had returned.

In retrospect I realise that this was the 'gift of faith' in operation. He had been graced with it where, in that particular instance, I had not. A few weeks later I found myself in a similar situation. A young married woman, who was in severe pain, came for prayer. A consultant to whom she had been referred had diagnosed three small growths on the cornea of her eye. She was to return the following week while he decided whether to treat it by the use of a laser beam, or to perform surgery.

While Sue was telling me this, there rose in my heart an inner confidence that God would heal her, and when we came to pray, I simply said, 'In the name of Jesus, be healed.' A warmth flowed into the side of her face and dispelled the pain. As arranged, she returned to the consultant and reported an abatement of the pain. The consultant was surprised because the growths were still there. Two weeks later the growths had gone completely and all that remained were three little scars.

John Hughes, one-time curate at Chorleywood, is now vicar of St Andrew's, Hatters Lane, a housing estate on the edge of High Wycombe in Buckinghamshire. The church is set on the side of a hill; to the right is a small middle-class residential area, to the left a large council estate. God worked powerfully through John and the congregation began to outgrow their facilities. He saw that the real need was for a centre from which they could minister to the community's spiritual and social needs. An architect was engaged to create a building which would serve all the main needs of the church in the area. The plan that he produced was acclaimed by all, but the problem was the estimated cost – £750,000!

This was seemingly out of reach for a predominantly working-class congregation. However, after assessing the situation, John felt an inward certainty that God would have them go forward as a venture of faith. The gift of faith was coming into operation. Now the new church is nearly finished and only a few thousand pounds remain to be raised.

I received a similar gift of faith in regard to our church development scheme. With a growing congregation we found it necessary to provide more facilities for every aspect of our church's life. An architect drew up plans and an appeal was launched. However, as the months passed new needs were discovered and we ended up with a total bill of £250,000. The people's initial response was wonderful, but we were left for six months with a deficit of £55,000.

David Pytches was away ministering in America and it

had been arranged that I should stay at home. One of my
responsibilities was to arrange an evening during which the
new buildings would be dedicated. Two weeks before the
planned event I felt God giving me a growing burden
regarding the outstanding debt. This burden turned to a
deep conviction that God wanted the buildings to open free of
this debt and that He would supply the money.

I kept wondering how God could possibly supply such an
amount. Our committed families had already given £195,000
and it was obvious that some had already responded twice to
the appeal. Suddenly the word of God came to me. The next
Sunday I was to ask fifty-five people to covenant £5.00 a
week for four years.

That Sunday, as I gave out the notices, I told the congregation that we were still £55,000 off target and that after
the next hymn I would explain to them how God intended to
supply the money. When I said this there was laughter. But I
felt that God had said to me that the money was in the
congregation and all that was needed was for the Holy Spirit
to release it. I explained what we were going to do and then
asked everyone to close their eyes so that nobody could see
what was happening. After that I called upon the Holy Spirit
to work. I alone kept my eyes open, and as I watched I could
see that many were being moved as God challenged them. I
then asked for a show of hands from those who were committing themselves. Gradually hands were raised and I counted
the numbers aloud. Twenty-seven hands went up.

On the Sunday evening I again told the congregation how
God would raise the money and again there were many
amused smiles. I then asked the Holy Spirit to complete His
work. Beginning counting at twenty-eight we went quickly to
forty and then stopped. We sat in silence for four or five
minutes, and during that time I felt the Lord was saying that
we needed to wait upon Him, as He had to do more work in
people's hearts before the rest of the money would be released. By the time we reached fifty-four, many were in tears,
and as the last hand rose the congregation broke into deafen-
ing applause in praise of God.

I felt God had given me a gift of faith for this £55,000. At no time during the Sunday did I doubt that all the money would be given, and I was able to speak that word with a God-given confidence. The result was a miracle!

It would seem that what differentiates the 'gift of healing' from a 'miracle' is that the latter is an immediate event. A miracle means 'an operation of power' and is a sign of the kingdom of God. I have seen miracles happen, both spontaneously within worship, and through the ministry of the laying on of hands with prayer.

At the end of a meeting we had led in Northern Ireland, I saw a lady, who had walked up from the back of the hall, sitting in the front obviously overcome with emotion. One moment tears were streaming down her cheeks, and the next she was laughing, bubbling over with great joy. She explained that for many years she had a wasting disease of the thigh and calf muscles. Besides the pain there was the visible deformity which caused some embarrassment. After a talk I had invited the Holy Spirit to work among us and during that time she had felt power moving rapidly throughout her wasting muscles. Very soon she discovered the diseased leg was as good as her other one.

When the apostle Paul was at Philippi preaching, he was distracted by a girl who earned her living as a fortune teller. Through the 'gift of the discerning of spirits' Paul saw that she was possessed by a spirit and cast it out (Acts 16:16–18).

At the start of a Saturday afternoon session held on the premises of Lisburn Cathedral I became particularly aware of the presence of a well-built young man in the congregation. His hair was dark and styled in a crew cut, but what particularly drew my attention to him was his eyes. These appeared to be just slits so that the pupils were hardly visible at all. I sensed, in the Spirit, that there was something demonic attached to him. Somehow I felt quite repulsed by him. During the ministry time I noticed he was in the queue of people waiting to be prayed for. The Bishop of Singapore had joined our team for that weekend and I thought I would make sure that the Bishop prayed for him when his turn

came. I turned my back on the queue and continued to pray
with a man whose back the Lord had just begun to heal. After
what I thought was a long enough period for the Bishop to
have taken him on, I turned to minister to the next person
and found myself looking straight at the very man I had
hoped to avoid.

My apprehension was entirely unfounded. The Holy
Spirit came powerfully upon his body and he shook violently.
I commanded all evil to leave him in the name of Jesus. At
this he sensed a rush from within and sank to the floor, where
he lay prostrate, breathing heavily. His friend knelt with him
and I gave instructions that he was not to be touched, but that
the Spirit of God, who was still obviously working on him,
must be allowed to do His own work. An hour later I met him
over a cup of tea. His eyes were clear and sparkling, and he
told me that something had left him. He said that he had
never felt so free in all his life!

I have always enjoyed reading books by missionaries who
recount the wonderful ways in which they experienced God
working in Africa or India. Among other things, they describe answered prayer, healings, and freedom from evil
spirits. I used to think that God only worked through such
devoted and dedicated people. However, I came to realise
that the key to His working was the Holy Spirit. It was not
until I knew His release that what I have described gradually
started to happen.

Chapter 4

'BE FILLED WITH THE SPIRIT'

One morning, whilst a curate in Camborne, I was sitting in my study when God began to speak to me in a rather unusual way. I felt He was telling me that during the morning I would experience an attack from a person, which would not be physical but spiritual. When this happened I was not to retaliate but simply to listen without comment. I was just bewildered and wondered whether the thought was just a flight of my imagination. Then about eleven o'clock the door bell rang and as I went to answer it I sensed the Lord telling me that this was the moment.

Standing on the doorstep was a relatively young man in a clerical collar. We hadn't met before, but I knew him to be a fervent evangelical. I invited him in and he gave me a broad, disarming smile. We went into my study with a cup of coffee and he told me that he wanted to come to the point. He said he believed that I was teaching erroneous doctrine concerning the Holy Spirit. For the next forty minutes he lectured me as if I had committed the unpardonable sin and I think that, had he been God, I would have been consigned to the fires of hell. By the time he had finished, my knees were shaking like jelly and I was fighting the temptation to give him one on the nose!

He found me biblically unsound on two points: the first was to do with the term 'baptism in the Spirit'. He said I was encouraging Christians to seek a 'second blessing' and there was no scriptural basis for that. He felt particularly annoyed because a number of his young people said that they had been blessed in this way through my ministry. His second point was that it was heretical to encourage people to speak in tongues because the gifts of the Spirit were withdrawn at the termination of the apostolic age. His Biblical exegesis, along with his knowledge of church history, left me somewhat bewildered. He ended up by telling me that he had already spoken about this problem with my vicar and warned him against the divisive nature of my ministry.

When he left I sat down exhausted but after overcoming my anger I realised that we were probably both wrong. My understanding of the work of the Holy Spirit had come through my experience. I had received the Holy Spirit and the gift of tongues seven years after I had received Christ. I identified this experience with what had happened to the believers in Samaria, who had received Christ through the preaching of Philip and the Holy Spirit through the ministry of Peter and John. Subsequently the way I taught people about the Holy Spirit began to change.

The reason I had had no release of the power of God and no gifts of the Spirit at my conversion was simply because nobody had told me about such possibilities. I now started to tell those I led to Christ that they needed to do a number of things. Firstly, to confess all known sins to Christ; then believe that He is alive and able to forgive. Next I explained the gift of tongues and encouraged the person to welcome the Holy Spirit into his heart as I prayed for him. I assured him that as I did this God would give him a 'worship language'.

However, many people still come to talk with me about their lack of spiritual power and reality. I have found that telling them to read the Bible, or pray more, is not really the answer, although both these practices are important for all disciples of Christ. Rather, I talk about what we actually possess through faith in Christ.

Two statements of Jesus have been especially helpful to me in this context. He said that the Spirit which He gave would be a spring welling up from within the believer's heart (John 4:14). Taking the same metaphor further, He said this would become a river of living water which would flow out from within (John 7:38). If this hasn't already been the seeker's experience, then I ask the Holy Spirit simply to release His life within, and I teach that this needs to be a continuous experience.

It would seem to me that being filled with the Spirit is allowing the life of Jesus to dominate and motivate every area of our lives. This is easy to write about and even easier to say, but for it to happen we need to be willing to obey the revelations and promptings of the Holy Spirit. He is the One who points out the blockages in our lives and He requires our response and willingness to have them dealt with.

One of the main ways of quenching the Spirit is having wrong attitudes to people. I have found this to be true in my own life, and it is equally true in the life of the congregation. In the early seventies we appointed what became known as the '1975 Committee'. Their brief was to study the present needs of all departments of the church's life, and try to project how these needs would alter during the next decade. Eventually they produced the long awaited report. One of the major recommendations was that we build new facilities, which would include a lounge and other buildings, to meet the need of the growing children's and young people's work.

This report caused a major division. Those who opposed the scheme argued that such exorbitant sums of money, if raised, should be given to the missionary societies and not spent on ourselves. Eventually the scheme was whittled down to a lounge in which to gather informally and to welcome new people. Even this was opposed – a number of strong personalities felt that the home was the place for entertaining and not the church.

The annual meeting of that year reached an all time low, when representatives stood up and argued their cases angrily. A few years later Eddie Gibbs selected St Andrew's as a model for research into church growth. He later showed us graphs to illustrate the way the church had grown since the renewal. He also showed us a diagram of our yearly giving. This, like numerical growth, had improved annually except for one year which revealed a decline. He asked if we could provide any explanation. Yes indeed! That was the year of bitterness by which, unknown to Eddie Gibbs, we had quenched the Holy Spirit in our hearts and fellowship.

During this unfortunate period I had always felt that the blame lay with those who opposed the proposed plan. If they had not been so arrogant and obstinate the fellowship would not have suffered. I also sensed how deeply this opposition had hurt John Perry, and this made me feel very angry. At the height of the controversy I took a day off and went up into the Chilterns to seek the Lord. He didn't speak to me about the rights or the wrongs of the particular scheme, rather about my own heart and attitude. The wrongs were within me and that was what was grieving the Holy Spirit.

For most of that year my ministry had seemed barren and my preaching shallow and critical. I was for ever sharing from the epistles of Paul how wrong attitudes damage a church's life and teaching that the only way forward was through repentance. However, the repentance I had in mind was not mine, but theirs! Eventually the truth dawned on me. I repented and then realised how far I had distanced myself from the life of the Spirit.

From my second year at theological college I had thought of myself as God's second gift to the Church of England. I was often invited by tutors to accompany them on their evangelistic engagements and to give a testimony. When the college outreach teams were selected for week-long missions I was normally included. If youth clubs phoned the college, requesting a speaker for an after-church meeting on a Sunday, or a houseparty, I was often recommended. It was tentatively suggested that when the time came to be ordained I might be able to begin my ministry working with young people at a leading London church. I so much wanted to be known, and whenever a leading evangelical preacher came to the college I always made it my business to meet him and introduce myself. It was at college that I first heard of the Keswick Convention and I felt it could only be a matter of time before I took my predestined place on that platform!

When the Holy Spirit filled me and I started to exercise gifts of the Spirit, I knew I no longer had any hope of becoming a well-known evangelical. However, I now sought to make a name for myself amongst the charismatics. During my last year in Cornwall I was invited to speak in many centres, including Fountain Trust conferences. I saw my move to Chorleywood as a springboard to even greater success.

John Perry, my new vicar, was a keen sportsman and played squash regularly. Within a few months of our arrival he introduced me to the Northwood Squash Club. We usually had a game, then chatted over a sandwich and a pint of beer. One particular lunchtime we finished our set and made our way back to the changing rooms. Entering the rooms, we were overcome by the smell of vomit. It looked as if a player had eaten a business lunch before he came and lost the whole of it on the floor of the shower room. The culprit was nowhere to be seen and I had little sympathy – and said so. John's reaction was exactly the opposite. He was concerned about the person and wondered whether there was anything he could do for him. He then took a towel and began to clear up the mess.

God used this one act to speak volumes to me about my pride and self-centredness. John's way was the way of the Spirit. I understood afresh that Christ came not to be served but to serve. In order to do that, He had to become of no reputation; the exact opposite of what I was seeking for myself. I realised that God still had a great work to do in my heart. I accepted this, but in practice I found it very difficult to let God change me.

In the early days of Faith Sharing God was continually challenging me about my pride. I well remember going with a team to Anston, near Sheffield. When finalising the programme I felt that the Lord wanted my friend Roy Clayton to speak at the main evangelistic family service on the Sunday. I can still recall the tussle I experienced. I kept saying to myself, 'The reason the team was invited was because of my reputation and the people up there have never heard of Roy

Clayton.' After a while I reached a compromise. Roy could preach and after the final hymn I would invite the people to come forward for prayer to receive Christ. The Lord seemed to say that I must do no such thing, but sit in the congregation and pray for Roy.

Humbling myself in this area continues to be a struggle. I have to fight constantly to let go of my desire to be top man. Allowing a man to minister in my place was one thing, allowing a woman was even more difficult. We were leading a meeting in Northern Ireland. In my spirit I knew that God was going to bless people powerfully at the ministry times and I was looking forward to leading it. Shirley was leading the worship, and I signalled to her: 'One more song and over,' and started to pray quietly. To my absolute consternation the Lord told me that He wanted Prue to lead the ministry. Almost audibly I called out 'Who?'

God has always used me evangelistically and I came to refer to those who came to know Christ in my preaching as 'my' converts. I was very jealous of them and took great pleasure on different occasions in hearing them telling how they had come to know Christ and my part in it. God then started to use me in the healing ministry and people sought me out for prayer. Again a reputation was developing and people telephoned me from long distances seeking my advice.

Once, when we were coming home from holiday, we stayed for a few days with our friends John and Gay Perry at Lee Abbey where John was Warden. Early one morning I walked out alone to the tower and observation point. I opened the door to the tower and sat down in order to appreciate the incredible beauty of the sea on both sides of the peninsula. As I watched, the words of the psalmist came into my mind: 'Once God has spoken; twice have I heard this: that power belongs to God' (Ps. 62:11, RSV). These words broke me. I knew at that moment that it wasn't the power of God that filled me with awe and wonder, but rather it was the satisfaction I received from having an evangelistic and healing ministry. My attitude was hindering the reign of the Holy Spirit in my life. Once again in tears I sought forgiveness and a new beginning. Pride is a great impediment to the flow of the Holy Spirit from us to others.

Another problem I had was disobedience. I once lost contact with God for a whole year through an act of disobedience. As a young man in New Zealand it had always been my desire to own a sports car. I had never seen the one I fancied in New Zealand, but had read up all the technical data and studied its photograph in magazines. I arrived in England with only £5, but I soon got work on building sites and amassed enough cash to buy the coveted MG. I started to look in the papers and soon came across a car which had one owner and was in mint condition. A visit to London, and I had made a commitment to buy. That evening I asked the Lord what He thought about it and He said quite plainly, 'No.' I had only been a Christian a few years and had never before experienced such an immediate response to prayer. For three days I had an incredible tussle with my conscience and having subdued it successfully went ahead with the purchase. The year that followed was full of crises and I was fortunate not to lose my life when, going into a corner at high speed, the car went spinning down the road completely out of control. This, God knew, would break my rebellion.

Mary and I have an extremely happy and fulfilling marriage. For eleven years now I have been travelling, which has meant many months away from her and the children. This ministry has only been possible because, from the beginning, we were both agreed that this was God's will for us. God has taken me to faraway places, thousands of miles from home, with temperatures and travelling conditions that seemed intolerable. On one occasion in India I lay on my bed filled with self-pity. My room in the conference centre was above a kitchen. A strong smell of curry and smoke filled it. If I opened the door to let in some air, the stench of the toilets was appalling. The heat was intense and the only water came from a filthy shower which dripped constantly from morning till night. I thought of Mary and the family at home and was angry with God for calling me to this ministry.

In such situations one cannot run home, and so I put an

end to my bout of self-pity and forced myself to recall the visions by which the Lord had brought me to where I was. In one of these I had been standing on a hill and before me, to the right, was a field of ripened grain which was bounded by the road. In front, another field stretched to the horizon which merged into purple hills. When this faded, I saw a sphere on which the continents of the world appeared. The Lord was commissioning me: 'You shall receive power when the Holy Spirit comes upon you and you shall be my witness in Jerusalem, and in all Judea and Samaria and to the end of the earth' (see Acts 1:8). The Lord brought back the vision of my call so clearly. The fields ready to harvest were stretched across the continents of the world. I confessed my rebellious-ness and self-pity, and the Lord began once again to restore me with his life through the Spirit.

Such experiences have led me to caution people who think God may be calling them to join us in our ministry teams. I usually say that it is possible God is calling them, but I describe in detail what the commitment entails and then suggest that they go away and pray about it. It is only if they still hear God calling that I will invite them to join with us. If God has not called, when the first major problem confronts us, we will want to run home.

In the ministry of the Holy Spirit one is always struggling over obedience to God. I was once invited to speak at the mid-week meeting of a Baptist church in preparation for a future Faith Sharing weekend. Some fifty members gathered to hear me describe our ministry. It was a happy time. Our sharing together was positive and constructive. I was asked to close the evening with a prayer and I was just about to do so when the Lord spoke to me.

I felt He wanted to heal a man in the congregation, unknown to me, who as a two-year-old had nearly drowned in a swimming pool. This accident had left him not just frightened of water, but also with a general fear in many areas of his life. I knew the Lord wanted me to say this, but it seemed so ridiculous and too embarrassing. 'Supposing I've just made it up,' I thought. 'Or, again, even though it is true, the person might not own up!' As I struggled with these thoughts I could sense the people wondering why I was not closing in prayer as requested. I cleared my throat and managed to speak out what I thought the Lord had told me. To my great relief a young West Indian man walked up to the front and said it was him. I prayed for his release and healing. On a subsequent visit to his home he shared how his life had been transformed from the moment of that prayer.

A working-class community is one thing; a cosmopolitan upper-class grouping is quite another. The chaplain of St Mark's, Maison Lafitte, invited me to take a Faith Sharing team to Paris for a ten day mission. In preparation I flew over and met a combined gathering of St Mark's congregation and people from another church under the chaplain's charge at Versailles. In the suburbs north of Paris there are some 20,000 English families, many of whom are employed by the giant international business corporations which have their headquarters there.

Because of the distances involved, a hall was hired for the evenings about mid-way between both churches. As I walked in I caught the atmosphere immediately. The predominant accent was public school and the many smooth collars sported university and regimental ties. Besides the business-men there were Embassy people. I was greeted warmly and they responded enthusiastically to the type of outreach proposed. Everything had been very English – so tactful, polite and decent. Then the Lord began to speak to me and I froze in my shoes.

I sensed Him telling me that there were a number present who were ready to respond to the gospel message and only needed an opportunity to receive Christ. I took one look at their faces and thought just how counter-productive an invitation to stay behind would be. It would be much better to wait until the mission was under way and I had my team around me! Then I could let it all happen. After all, the purpose of that evening's gathering was solely to share the vision of the coming mission with the two churches. I was thinking along these lines when the chaplain asked me if I would close the official part of the evening with prayer.

I stood in silence, knowing the Lord had spoken, but terrified of the consequences if I obeyed: it seemed such a foolish thing to say. Finally, with a pounding heart I announced that, after the meeting, I was putting a row of chairs near where I was standing and if there were any seeking God and wanting prayer, they should come forward and sit on one of them. After the prayer I kept my eyes closed and stayed where I was, just hoping the floor would open and swallow me up. Then I sensed some shuffling and to my amazement I found, on peeping through my fingers, that all the seats had been taken. Amongst those who came that evening was an Italian, Arturo, who was a manager with an international company. The chaplain, Alan Lindsay, had recently visited his home in connection with the baptism of his son. Arturo's wife, Lesley, had, after lengthy questioning, come to the place where she definitely wanted to become a Christian. Arturo, on the other hand, had held off, thinking it was all rather personal and unnecessary as he was a baptised Roman Catholic. However that evening he had sensed God working in his life and suddenly began to want God desperately.

It has not always been like this. Many times courage has failed me completely and I have gone home with a great sorrow in my heart. This is particularly true of personal witness. I was sitting with a couple on a train and the wife was saying how she would love to be able to go on a package holiday, but the thought of flying filled her with fear. I felt the Lord telling me to pray for her. We have often done this for people with this problem in our ministry in churches, but here on a train courage failed me and I went home feeling sad that I had disobeyed the Lord and quenched His Spirit.

At college there was a fellow student who used to make me so cross that I avoided him whenever possible. He apparently felt called to be the tester of the spiritual temperature of the college. He had a knack of sidling up at breakfast and asking what God had been saying during one's early morning 'quiet time'. This was a catch-22 situation. If you replied 'nothing', then a lecture would follow over the toast and marmalade about your hardness of heart. On the other hand, if you confided a spiritual thought, he would analyse it and suggest ways of responding in obedience to God. He always carried a well-marked Bible, and used it so much that it had to be replaced every year.

For all his awkwardness he had grasped a crucial lesson – the need to practise a discipline in our relationship with Christ. It is through the word of God that His Spirit speaks and gives us our resources. I have always had to fight for this time each day as there are always so many other things demanding my attention. When business does get the better of me, I dry up inside like a prune and it is only by reverting to the discipline of scriptural meditation and prayer that my spirit can fill up again with the water of life.

I find that any breakdown in this discipline has a subtle effect on other areas of my life also. Food is good and a gift from God. But too much food leads to gluttony and this gradually erodes spirituality. During one period of my life my prayers had become just routine and when I did pray it involved a hasty few verses and a prayer. I became listless and was forever eating whatever was available. At our main evening meal I usually ended up with a second helping from both courses as well as scraping out the bowl. New Zealanders are weaned on beer and I was no exception. However, I found I was undisciplined in my drinking habits and, with the combination of the extra food, I added over a stone to my weight.

I know what it is like to play rugby when unfit, especially in the fly-half position. After a series of runs and the odd tackle my heart would pound so much that I felt it was going to explode in my chest. Indiscipline causes spiritual unfitness and allows the basic instincts to dominate life. The times I have known special anointings of the Spirit have been those when I had been practising a disciplined life.

When the lower instincts dominate we get a bad conscience and we ask the Lord to forgive and help us. This, in itself, doesn't really change the situation because we soon repeat our self-indulgences. What we need to do is, after confession, to renounce the hold which a particular indulgence has on us and ask the Holy Spirit to release and fill us. In the case of my inordinate appetite for food this prayer proved a turning point for me. I went back to a healthy weight and the Holy Spirit's power was renewed within me.

I have always identified with Timothy, St Paul's protégé and colleague. Apparently he was rather a fearful sort of person and Paul had to remind him of the nature of the Holy Spirit's work. According to Paul He is a Spirit of love, power and self-control (2 Tim. 1:7). Before experiencing the filling of the Holy Spirit I had little concept at all of the holiness of God. My concern was more for who I was and what I did. As I entered more fully into worship and glimpsed a little of the majesty of God, I became fearful, but it was the wrong kind of fear. It was not that I was in awe of God, but rather frightened of Him. At the root of this fear was the overriding thought that God might ask me to do something I didn't want to do, such as living in a mud hut in Africa, serving Him in the forests of Borneo, or taking my family from me. I struggled with this for many months whilst the fear quenched the life of God's Spirit within me. In seeking help from friends I discovered my need for more inner healing.

Just after I had arrived in England I had experienced a period of great anxiety. I felt a call to the ordained ministry but did not even have the necessary 'O' and 'A' level examinations. This meant that I had to work in a factory or labour on a building site during the day to maintain myself whilst I studied in the evenings. Doubts about my ability to pass, and uncertainty about my future if I failed, caused my stomach to become so sore that I began to experience difficulty keeping my food down, and doctors detected a duodenal ulcer.

The Holy Spirit was hindered from having a free rein in my heart by my anxiety. This caused me to start taking seriously the teaching of Jesus about anxiety. In the Sermon on the Mount He told His disciples not to be anxious. Paul re-echoed His words with an exhortation to pray to God about those situations which cause the anxiety state. I developed a discipline for clearing the 'in-tray' of my mind. Each anxious thought is daily brought to Christ and discussed fully with Him. As I did this, my worries gradually disappeared and peace was restored.

I find that being filled with the Spirit is both a state and an experience. Through my prayer time each day I seek to put right any relationship or attitudes which are not of God. Where necessary I humble myself and ask forgiveness. I know that there are many unknown wrongs also and I ask God to cleanse me from these through the blood of Jesus which He shed for us all on the cross of Calvary. As far as possible I try to be at one with Jesus so that His peace can pervade my life. To maintain this state it is necessary to bring to him all that comes across my path during the day.

On occasions I have known a different experience of the Holy Spirit filling me. Whilst engaged in worship I sometimes sense heat in my body, or a fullness in my chest which feels as if it is being blown up like a balloon. At times, when I pray for healing, or prophesy, I feel I am being immersed physically into a pool of the most incredible love. These are all variations of the Holy Spirit's anointing, which may come when one is open to God. However, His major ministry is to make Jesus known and we are finding this in ever greater degrees as we spend time in worship.

Chapter 5

THE WORSHIP OF GOD

Before His death Jesus told His disciples that when He was raised He would meet them again in Galilee. True to His word, He appeared and in response they worshipped Him. Because of the ways in which the Holy Spirit is working He is making Jesus more real, and believers want to respond to Him in new ways. As a result many congregations are discovering the joys, and traumas of worshipping God.

Ever since I can remember, the beauty of the creation has moved me greatly. Camping in the bush as a teenager I would often lie on my back at night staring into the heavens. The sparkling canopy never ceased to fill me with a sense of awe and wonder. I had experienced the same emotions when watching the sun rise over the mountains or sink over the Pacific Ocean. Long before I knew Christ my heart responded in worship. Unfortunately, when I first attended church as a committed Christian what happened there failed to create a similar response.

A few years ago, I was invited to lead a New Year's houseparty for University College, London. For a number of years I had spoken regularly at their weekly Thursday Communion Service held in the hall of a church in Tottenham Court Road – a place made famous by George Whitefield, the revivalist preacher. The Christian undergraduate leadership at the university had abandoned a rather inflexibie attitude and decided to create an open fellowship to which Christians of all persuasions, and people with none, could gather together and explore their faith. Malcolm Rushton, the chaplain, had developed a delightful service of worship based on the Lord's Supper. Besides the instrumentalists and singers, he encouraged spontaneity in prayer and was open for the Holy Spirit to minister His gifts. It was obvious that the students related to this form of worship as the large hall was always packed whenever I visited. Malcolm kindly invited me to lead a houseparty and I knew that we would have a great time with the Lord together.

Four days together with 160 students allows sufficient time for friendships to be made and masks to be taken down. It had been decided that on the final Sunday evening we would have a Communion service in the chapel after supper. By the time washing up was finished it was after eight o'clock. The service began with songs of praise. Malcolm spoke, and we prayed before sharing the bread and wine, then we just continued to worship. During this period opportunity was given for those who wanted prayer to kneel at the Communion rails. I looked around to see what was happening and noticed that people were either standing or sitting to worship or kneeling for prayer. I had been praying with people for some time and my legs were beginning to ache. I looked at my watch to see what time it was, only to discover that I had left it in my room, so I asked Malcolm. To our amazement, he said 3.00 a.m.! We had been worshipping the Lord for seven hours!

Such experiences become possible only when the great majority of those involved are wanting to worship God in that particular way. However, it is much more difficult introducing such worship to an Anglican parish church. New patterns of worship evolve gradually and changes must first begin in our hearts. God enables us to worship in depth by giving us His Spirit and particularly the prayer of tongues – a gift which has been the focus of so much controversy. For many Christians 'tongues' is their first encounter with something which cannot be understood or explained satisfactorily through the intellect.

We were once visiting a church with a Faith Sharing team. At the end of the evening service many people came forward for prayer, whilst others stayed in the pews talking quietly together or praying. Slowly the church started to empty. By about 9.30 p.m. the only people left were our team and a young wife who was sitting in the front row with her head held between her hands. I asked her name and whether we could help. She replied that her name was June, and she was very afraid, but was ready. Firstly I prayed that God's love would cast this fear from her. She immediately relaxed and sat up. Then, sensing that the Lord wanted to gift her with tongues, I suggested that she receive it. On mentioning this, she suddenly became quite hostile. She told me in no uncertain terms that she didn't believe in tongues.

June's indoctrination against 'tongues' had started just after she received Christ. In her previous church she had been taught that the gifts of the Spirit belonged to the first century, but had ceased with the writing of the New Testament and were not for today. Her vicar had counselled her to beware of people who claimed to have such experiences today as they were deceived by the devil. I let her talk like this for some time and then said that although she might not believe in tongues, God did and He wanted her to have this gift. It was as if her talking about her unbelief released it from her for within a few minutes of my praying she was speaking fluently in an unknown language.

'Wycliffe' is a famous centre near High Wycombe where missionaries are taught the science of linguistics in order to translate the Bible into the language of the people to whom they go. We led a church weekend which was based on this centre and which some of the resident staff attended. I prayed for a delightful young couple, Philip and Liz, and the Lord healed Philip of severe epilepsy. Whilst praying for him, I saw the Holy Spirit resting on Liz and encouraged her to speak in tongues.

She found the whole idea extremely difficult. As a professional linguist she was fluent in three languages, which she had learned, but she could not understand how God could possibly give a language to a person which had never been learned. Her mind was buzzing with questions. One was: would anyone be able to understand what was being said? I was able to tell her about a Nigerian lady doctor who came to our church for the Sunday service. At the ministry time she asked for prayer. Our deaconess, Margaret, and two friends prayed over her. Not knowing what more to pray, Margaret continued praying softly in tongues. She then spoke to the Nigerian lady who said, 'Yes, that was what I understood Margaret to say earlier'! Margaret was most surprised; she had been totally unaware that she had been communicating with her in her native tongue.

I told Liz that this was a less common experience in the use of tongues, but that the main use was for private worship. When praying for the release of this gift in someone I have often found it helpful, if I sense the Lord prompting me, to introduce it in the following way. Firstly, I invite the Holy Spirit to come upon the person, and then ask Him to impart the gift of tongues. I then tell the person that I am going to touch his lips and when I do that he is to speak his new language. This is not a formula, but it creates a situation where faith can be applied. This was the case with Liz.

When this prayer gift is imparted, some satanic attack may follow, often coming in the form of doubt. A whispering voice insists that one is making it up, or it is meaningless. I have found that few people escape such initial temptations and I always encourage them to keep using what God has given.

Each morning when I come before the Lord, I start simply by worshipping Him through this prayer language. I find it helpful to remind myself that I am speaking to God and the essence of what I am saying is a mystery. In my worship I have found this gift to be like a 'booster rocket' that takes my prayers out of the mind and into the spirit. The more I seek to express my love for Jesus the more I am conscious of my mind's inability to express what I feel within my heart. The gift of tongues helps particularly in this area. Often I find that the end of such worship is silence. I pray or sing in tongues for a time and then I am still. This seems to take away tension and prepare my spirit to wait upon God. Then my worship continues in my own language, interspersed with tongues as I seek to respond to what I feel God has been saying to me in the stillness.

We learn to worship in this way on our own; then we can join together with others in a cell or house meeting. Any difficulties people are having with the worship in the church will be represented in this group. The progress of a group depends on how far each member is prepared to open his life to God in the fellowship. Some feel that a Bible study and formal prayer is the extent of their commitment, while others would add the ingredients of sharing, prayer for one another, and worship in various degrees. A group is often prevented from becoming a worshipping fellowship by reserve on the part of the members, often the result of unresolved emotional traumas.

It is part of our British culture to deny our emotions. We are taught from an early age that boys don't cry and in situations of great sorrow and grief we are expected to keep a stiff upper lip. Within many of us there are unexpressed hurts and fears which the personal presence of the Holy Spirit touches upon when we worship. Worship is like making love. St Paul sets the relationship of the risen Christ with His people in a marriage context by calling the church 'The Bride of Christ'. For love-making to be truly an exchange of love, outstanding grievances must be settled and assurances of love and commitment must be given. It is the same when Christ, the Bridegroom, draws near to us. As we experience His love we offer our whole person to Him without reservation and He fills our hearts with His spirit. In the beginning I was unable to deal with God at such close quarters and would leave meetings early in order to miss the worship. Then one evening I summoned up the courage to ask other members of the group to pray for me. I knelt on the floor whilst they laid hands on me and prayed. One fringe member was extremely angry at this and decided never to come back to the group again. Thankfully through another group he was later helped to deal with the emotional problems which praying for me had brought to the surface within him.

If the members of a group are not prepared to tackle these real problems within themselves, then the group will either stagnate or die. Mary and I had a sad experience of the death of a group. We had collected together ten or twelve people who had either just become Christians or were just about to do so. Our aim was, with God's help, to enable the group to become an informal gathering where they could worship, receive teaching, and find healing. To start with, it was wonderful. Members committed their lives to Christ, and others seemed to be growing in their faith. Then we hit trouble. We began to touch on unresolved problems within each other and unfortunately there was not the desire to seek healing. People began making excuses for not turning up – a number gave business commitments as their reason, others lack of time. Eventually we shrank to four and on two occasions there was only Mary and myself. With a sense of failure we accepted that the group was finished.

However, such a group as I have described can work through their problems together and become a worshipping people. Our latest home group is doing just that. Jim, our leader, made worship his first priority and gently encouraged us to respond to the Lord. We begin our time together with one of our number leading in worship on the guitar. The songs are interspersed with short prayers of thanksgiving and praise. We share from the Scriptures and pray for each other. I have found it helpful to worship the Lord and listen to Him in private before the meeting in order that, when we meet corporately, I have a contribution to make.

There is a story of a rabbi who was about to retire. The local merchants all decided to give him a large barrel of wine as a leaving present. They agreed to send the barrel on a cart to each of their premises so that each merchant could pour in his contribution. The full barrel was subsequently presented to the rabbi with many speeches. When the rabbi came to draw off the first draught of wine, he found that it was only water. Each contributor had thought that if he gave water it would pass unnoticed in the general sharing. The quality of worship depends on what each member is able to contribute. Having said that, there will be times when, for some reason or other, we are unable to contribute much and that is the time when the rest can minister to us.

In a worship service it is important to be clear about the leadership. For one thing, this makes the people feel more secure. My most embarrassing time in this connection was just after David Pytches had arrived to be our vicar. We had decided to hold a half-night of prayer which included periods of worship, followed by meditation on the Scriptures. We duly gathered at eight, sang a spiritual song or two, and waited in silence. We don't mind silence, but this seemed strangely uncomfortable. As the evening went on it got progressively worse until, by 10.30 p.m., we were all glad to call it a day. David asked me later what I thought had gone wrong. I suggested that it was probably in the leadership. Maybe, being new, he had not wanted to exert too much direction! He looked at me in amazement and said that he thought he had made it plain that I was meant to be leading it!

Worship begins in the heart and may be shared with others in small groups. The most difficult part is introducing it into the Sunday services. Most clergy, choir members and organists have been involved in the worship of the church since childhood. They know their job – chanting psalms, singing anthems and hymns and reciting prayers. They have rehearsed the ways in which the worship leaders should enter the building and the attitudes they should adopt once inside. They feel secure with these traditional, familiar forms of worship. No wonder one organist complained bitterly that our Faith Sharing music style was hurdy-gurdy and belonged to the fair.

John Perry, one of the most loving and patient pastors I have known, had the task in the early days at St Andrew's of introducing songs of renewal to the worship of the church. Many had already become familiar with these in their home groups. One of our Faith Sharing musicians had written a

folk setting for the Communion Service. We used this effec-
tively in many churches where we were invited for Faith
Sharing, but we were still experiencing opposition to the new
work of the Spirit in St Andrew's. People were unwilling to
learn any new songs and we reached stalemate.

John felt that the way of love was not to insist, but to pray
and wait for a change. Eighteen months went by, the choir
dwindled to four or five faithfuls and, except for a few songs,
nothing new was happening in the worship of the church.
There was a wail of discontent amongst those who longed to
go forward. Much against his will, John decided to close
down the choir for a month.

Margaret had a beautiful singing voice and was in sympathy with the type of worship which we were seeking to
introduce to the congregation. John made her the new choir
leader and after a month reconstituted the choir. Soon some
twenty-five new singers joined. From day one she laid down
as first priority the need to pray together before leading
worship. They began to seek God before each rehearsal and
for half-an-hour before each Sunday service. The effect upon
the congregation was spiritually creative.

John Wimber, a personal friend of David and Mary
Pytches, invited them to stay with him in California for a
holiday. One of the first things David said to me when he
came back was that we had more to learn about worship.
This came as rather a shock because I thought that we had
learned a lot! He said that he believed that in worship we
should be seeking to touch the heart of God with our
adoration and praise.

By this time Margaret and her husband were moving to
London and Geoff was taking over the leadership of the
choir. David had brought back some recordings of the songs
and the choir began to include some of these in our worship,
though they had difficulty with them. Some were love songs
to Jesus, using intimate terms lovers use, others focussed
on the objective qualities of the Godhead. There was less
explicit teaching in them and a lot of repetition.

We listened carefully to our critics, but felt this type of

worship was being rejected for the wrong reasons. The fact that intimacy and repetitiveness in worship caused embarrassment was no reason for holding back. When lovers are together, they don't tell each other once of their love, but many times. The words of human love are repetitive and so can be the words of those seeking to love the Lord their God with all their heart, mind and soul.

The next step was a crucial one. If we were going to take this type of worship seriously, then we had to make space for it within the liturgy and not confine it to a couple of songs. We asked Geoff to prepare six or eight worship songs and to sing them straight through, repeating some if he felt inclined. During this time we told the congregation that they could either kneel, sit or stand. The songs were not introduced individually. At first the numbers were included on the hymn board. Later the songs were projected on to a large screen.

Over a period of time it became noticeable that however we worshipped it was invariably followed by silence. Sometimes the singers and musicians started with songs of praise which led into the love songs. At other times the process was reversed. If the worship ended on a paean of praise, the congregation would often continue singing in tongues and then would come silence.

Silences cause as much of a problem for some people as intimate worship does for others. Some couldn't cope with silence at first and would try to fill the time with a text of Scripture, a prayer or a song. Before worship began we used to tell the congregation that there was no need to say anything, but just to relax and listen to God. Sometimes the silence is broken by God as someone prophesies or speaks in tongues. We have a rule that only members of our church may exercise the gifts of the Spirit in our worship as we have to be accountable for what is done and if anything is said that we feel to be questionable then we can discuss it with the person concerned afterwards. Speaking in tongues has the effect of creating expectancy as, again, in the silence we pray for an interpretation. Periodically we explain at that point what has happened so that new people understand. If an interpretation is not immediately forthcoming, we encourage the person who has been given it to speak out. This is useful because sometimes it is a young Christian who has been given it and he may have difficulty in speaking publicly.

Sometimes an individual may sing in tongues, and the person with the interpretation may be led to sing it with the same tune, or speak it. Following Paul's advice to the Corinthians, we limit prophecies to a maximum of three at a time, and the same with tongues.

God uses prophecies to encourage the whole congregation, but often they have a personal application. For some people a prophecy confirms what God has been saying to them. When I was a student I once heard the late Pastor Richards of the Slough Pentecostal Church say that as a teenager he felt that God was calling him to the full time ministry. A number of people had confirmed this to him, but he asked God if He would confirm it through prophecy. In his prayer he promised God that, if He did, then he would never question Him again on the matter. On the Sunday night he went down to the church and hid under the Communion table which was draped with a large heavy cloth. During the service there was a prophecy which confirmed everything about which he felt God had been speaking to him.

During the course of a conducted tour round Pastor Richard's church I was led into an empty carpeted room. When I asked what it was for, I was told it was the 'waiting room'. It was there, before evening worship, that the leadership waited for the anointing power of the Holy Spirit. David had the same thought when he started prayer meetings in our Upper Room three quarters of an hour before our services. These were open to the worship leaders and anyone else who cared to join with us. They provided an opportunity for those who were leading the worship to be in tune with God before the service began.

At times I have arrived agitated, having had a disagreement with the children, or a difficult phone call from a disgruntled parishioner. In the waiting atmosphere of this meeting, difficulties can be resolved and the inner freedom

restored without which it is impossible to worship or lead
worship.

Mary and I were once at a party organised by the hospice
where she is a Clinical Teacher. During the evening I fell into
conversation with one nursing officer who told me that
although she is not from our area she had been to our church
and had had what to her was a remarkable experience. For
many years she had suffered from a back problem. She had
originally hurt it as a student, lifting heavy patients. In order
to sit comfortably she had always to adopt a slanting position. When the time of open worship started she decided to
stay seated and was surprised when she felt the upper half of
her body being filled with heat. She tentatively eased herself
into a normal sitting position and discovered that she was
free of pain. She told me that on the way out she said to David
that something incredible had happened to her. He had
replied that such things were not unusual during the worship
time. This, as much as the healing, had amazed her.

The Psalmist tells us that God is enthroned upon the
praises of His people (Ps. 22:3, RSV). When the Lord is so
present, then spontaneous acts of compassion towards His
people as they worship are to be expected. Sometimes He
wishes his healing to be ministered through the gifts of the
Spirit and we have discovered that worship is the ideal
setting for releasing the gifts. When John Wimber first came
his team ministered words of knowledge during the
worship. Our problem was that it was an informal Saturday
night gathering and we did not then know how to take this
new freedom of worship over into a liturgical setting.

David decided to ask God for these gifts during the
worship time in the Upper Room before the service started.
Just before we went into the congregation he would also ask
the Father what He planned to do that morning or evening. If
God told any of us, we were encouraged to tell everyone in the
room, and David would make a list and read it out before the
final blessing at the end of the service. Like many others, I
was at first rather sceptical of this innovation, but something
happened which was to change my mind completely.

Before one evening service one of those waiting on the Lord said that at the service there would be a mother and small baby who would be travelling up from Surrey and the Lord intended to heal the baby from a particular ailment. My immediate thought was that babies are never brought to the evening worship. I well remember taking a walk around the congregation to see if I could spot this supposed baby. My scepticism was confirmed. At the end of the service David read out the words and some of us remained at the communion rail to pray with those who came forward in response. Imagine my surprise when apparently from nowhere a young mother stood before us with a little baby in her arms. She had come up from Surrey. Surprise turned to amazement when some weeks later it was reported back that the baby had been healed.

Introducing words of knowledge caused quite a stir in the congregation. Some felt it offensive and most unnecessary. I was inclined to agree, especially since at times it fell to my lot to have to read them out. I had to stand there announcing that there were special people that the Lord wanted to bless, such as a lady with a bruised left toe, a man with a swollen ankle, a man with a persistent headache, a woman with backache, and so on. It was most difficult.

The sceptics pointed out that in any given group of people there would be a number with aches in the body and pains in the head, etc. I silently agreed with all the criticisms, yet I could not deny what I saw happening before my eyes.

On one occasion a word was given that a man had jammed his little finger in the car door on his way to the service. And there he was! When he came forward, it was still throbbing. However, this wasn't the main thing the Lord wanted to do for him. He didn't know Christ and was astonished that God had actually been aware of such personal details about him. I was privileged to lead him to the cross and into a saving knowledge of Jesus Christ.

While things were evolving in this manner it became noticeable that people who were brought by friends, or were coming out of curiosity, were being spiritually awakened. As a result, a number were coming to know Christ. Brian and Jean came forward for prayer after one service. I asked them what they wanted Jesus to do for them. They had been moved by the love of the people and a sense of God's presence as people were engaged in worship. Although they still couldn't enter into the worship, they felt happy to be there. They wanted to know how they could discover the God who was obviously so real to the congregation.

Some years ago we took a Faith Sharing team to Southall, the Hindu centre of Europe. For this venture nearly all the local churches combined. Besides a number of public meetings, a hundred or so outreach meetings were held in private homes. During that time we became especially involved with Roy. He was an unmarried Anglican priest who had opened his house to the local skinheads. There were about thirty National Front black-hating young people. Much of the racial violence on the surrounding estates had been perpetrated by them. Half a dozen had been in prison and others were working out sentences by doing compulsory community service. I had taken Alf Cooper to one of the meetings in Roy's home. Alf and his wife Hilary were missionaries on leave from Chile who were staying in our parish while engaging in deputation work across the country. He shared the gospel with these young people and at the end we prayed with two or three who showed concern for their spiritual state.

I kept in contact with this group and when John Wimber returned to our church for a second time I invited them over. It was a Saturday night and I organised a number of cars to fetch them, taking them first to our home for tea. They had promised me that there would be no drink or drugs and they kept their word.

When we arrived at the church every seat was taken except the choir stalls which our wardens had reserved for them and John had started leading songs of worship from the piano. I held my breath as thirty skinheads in bovver boots and halfmast jeans pushed noisily forward and shoved each other into the seats. None to my knowledge had ever been to a church before, let alone to a middle class community. Seemingly unaware of what was happening, John and the team continued to lead us in the worship of God.

Suddenly all the girls rushed off to the loo like a stampeding herd of elephants. Their move was greeted by obscenities from the boys. Within ten minutes they were all back and started chatting to the boys again. Pete, who was sitting next to me, said he just had to go out for a fag, but would come back. When one of his friends enquired in a loud voice what he was doing, he and six others joined the exodus.

I sat red-faced. The perspiration was running in rivulets down my back. I had seen them rioting in Southall High Street and knew that, as a gang, they feared neither God nor man. The thought of some impending disaster was increased when they decided to sit on top of the choir stalls where the hymn books were kept. Whilst all this was taking place the congregation continued in worship and after about forty minutes a relative quietness descended. John started to minister in the gifts of the Spirit. A quarter of the group left to terrorise Chorleywood High Street, but the rest stayed put, fascinated by what was beginning to happen. Pete, who had a tattoo of a snake coming out of his ear, was rigid, apparently unable to move. Our people walked among them praying whenever they sensed the Holy Spirit was resting. During this I experienced an intensely sad moment.

Kathy, with tears in her eyes, asked me to pray for her. She was about seventeen, her head was shaved, and heavy make up covered her pretty face. I asked her what she would like prayer for. She replied simply that she wanted to have a baby. I enquired about her husband, but she said she was not married – in fact she didn't have a special boy friend, as she belonged to all the boys in the group. I talked to her about Jesus and the wonderful plans which He had for her life which could include marriage and a family. She told me that it sounded good, but she had never meant anything to anybody and wanted a baby so that she could have someone special for herself.

There was one particular boy who had just had the short

sharp custodial treatment which is supposed to reform young potential criminals. I had spoken with him about Jesus on a number of occasions when I was alone with him and he was quite open and interested. However, in the group he would sometimes become completely uncontrollable and destroy anything or anyone in his way.

I noticed during the worship that he became quite agitated, but stayed put and hovered around those who were being prayed for. John Wimber walked up to him and seemed just about to pray when he walked away again. John repeated this about twenty minutes later. In the Vicarage that evening I asked him why he hadn't prayed for him. He replied that he had seen what the problem was but couldn't pray because the Holy Spirit wasn't on the lad.

John's response puzzled me. However, what puzzles me more is why God was apparently unable to break into these lives and, by the power of His Spirit, give them a radical new beginning. Roy had loved them and made his home available twenty-four hours a day. He had spoken for them in court, and travelled long distances to visit them in prison. In a creative way he had presented the gospel to them and daily remembered them in his prayers. On that Sunday evening it would seem that a number were conscious of God, but then and subsequently they didn't want to do anything about it. In our ministry we are continually meeting such situations, and as yet we have found no answer.

Nothing reveals the state of our hearts more clearly than a Spirit-filled act of worship. As we seek to embrace God His Spirit touches the deep areas of our lives. If we have deep unresolved hurts or relationships worship can be a traumatic experience. However, if we allow God His way, it can lead to healing.

Chapter 6

HEALING THE BROKEN-HEARTED

In 1986 I was invited to take a Faith Sharing team to New Zealand. The prospect of this six-week tour filled me with great joy and anticipation. Except for an occasional visit to parents, which lasted a few weeks, I had not been back for twenty-four years.

Our first engagement was in Dunedin. I awoke early and went for a walk. Within half an hour I was walking through native bush, and climbing into the hills above the city. Suddenly I began to weep. This surprised me and I put it down to stress resulting from the journey and my forthcoming responsibilities.

Later on we went to Pigeon Bay opposite Akaroa Harbour and spent a day on a farm. In the morning we relaxed together and later in the day I climbed a hill at the back of the farm. Again I wept, but this time great sobs seemed to be coming from deep within my heart. I realised I was grieving, and the reason gradually dawned on me. When I left New Zealand it hadn't been my intention to stay away permanently. However, as my life and ministry developed in England, I had to suppress the deep feelings I had for my country and people. As a result an area of my heart was broken and needed the healing touch of the Holy Spirit. My grief had been triggered off by encountering again the beauty of the land and the way of life of my people.

Often such inner hurts surface during Spirit-filled worship. This is the reason why many find such worship difficult. It was early in my ministry that I realised how many people are hurt in this way. I was speaking at a meeting in the lecture theatre of a college. The subject I had been asked to take was 'The Ministry of Jesus'. For my introduction I had taken the Nazarene Manifesto where Jesus had said: 'The Spirit of the Lord is upon me, because he has anointed me to preach good news to the poor. He has sent me to proclaim freedom for the prisoners and recovery of sight for the blind, to release the oppressed, to proclaim the year of the Lord's favour' (Luke 4:18–19).

Although I sought to develop all the points Jesus was making, I had spent more of my time showing how Jesus healed the broken-hearted. The lecture theatre was rather cramped at the front, so I suggested that any who would like prayer should go to the chapel. This was a Victorian monstrosity which seemed to be almost as large as half the rugger pitch which was adjacent to it. By the time we arrived, the altar rail was full of kneeling students and between the choir stalls a large group stood in silence awaiting their turn for prayer. As we asked each one what they wanted prayer for it was soon obvious that the main problems were emotional. Many in their short lives had suffered in deep ways. We heard of fathers who had left their families, of young people who discovered that they were illegitimate, of parents who had abused them, of abortions, and so on.

Two young women – one looking like a zombie – came to the little team in which I was praying. Judith was about twenty-one, pretty, with her blonde hair swept back in a boyish cut. Her eyes were blank, and stared rather than looked at you. I asked her what she would like prayer for but she made no response. Her friend then stepped in and told us her story.

She had invited Judith, a Roman Catholic, to come with her to the meeting. During the previous day Judith had confided to her something which had happened nine years previously. When she was twelve her father and grandfather had both committed incest with her. The effect had been so traumatic that she had never been able to tell anyone. She felt guilty and unclean and couldn't have any physical contact with men – she even recoiled from shaking my hand. We gathered around her and asked the Holy Spirit to come and in Jesus' name to bind up her broken heart. She began to tremble all over. I encouraged her to invite Jesus into the memory of that horrific experience. She told us afterwards that it was at that point that she sensed an inner release followed by a vision of Jesus standing before her. Her first thought was that He was a man and she began to recoil. However, He stepped forward and simply embraced her in His arms. She felt relaxed. A feeling of intense love and cleansing filled her body. After we had finished praying, the transformation was immediate. Her eyes shone, she shared with us what had happened, and to cap it all she gave us all a hug!

The students at this meeting had all been born in the sixties when permissiveness had become more respectable. To keep abreast with what was happening in society, Parliament had passed laws on divorce, homosexuality, and abortion, which removed the old boundaries based on Christian revelation. The meeting illustrated yet again that many of our problems stem from emotional traumas.

I was sitting in our garden engrossed in a book one day when, looking up, I saw a young woman with a baby under the apple tree. We had first met her and her husband some twelve years before and, except for a couple of times, I had not seen them since. Anyone meeting Ann then would have noticed that she was very 'performance orientated' always saying and doing what she considered was expected of her. She suffered from chronic bad health. From her student nursing she acquired a back condition and every germ or virus seemed to make a bee-line for her. Periodically she became totally unable to cope. She was calling on us because her husband (who was a clergyman) had sent her away for a week to convalesce from her latest illness.

Ann's problems started on the day she was born. Her mother already had two daughters and with her next pregnancy had set her heart firmly on having a son. In fact, she had given her a boy's name which, for obvious reasons, I have not used. For the first six weeks her disappointed mother would have little to do with her, and could not bring herself to push the pram in public places. When she was twelve her father had died after a long illness. At about the same time her mother had told her that she had never wanted her and considered her nothing but a nuisance.

Not surprisingly this traumatic background had stamped her with deep feelings of rejection. Wherever she went she attempted to make herself lovable, but never felt that anyone ever really loved and accepted her in return. This applied to her husband, toddler, sisters and close friends, to say nothing of the numerous people she met in her husband's parish. It was obvious that she had a real faith in God, who, again, she was trying hard to please all the time. She could never be certain that Jesus accepted her. All her relationships, both human and divine, were coloured by this rejection.

As we waited upon the Lord, I sensed that one of the barriers that needed to be removed was anger and resentment which she held against her mother. I encouraged her to see her mother in her mind and consciously forgive her, going over the situations in which she had been hurt. When she had done that I reminded her that Jesus told us to bless our enemies and those who hurt us, and I asked her to pray God's blessing upon her mother. This prayer made it possible for her to experience Jesus in a most vivid way, accepting her at different periods of her life, beginning with her birth. Following this inner experience the pain in her back left her.

It is our experience that often severe physical illnesses are caused by what Jesus would term 'a broken heart'. On one occasion when I was ministering with a Faith Sharing team. I walked around the church during the prayer time observing what was happening. I stopped behind a young lady whose hands were strapped by leather supports but who I had noticed struggling up the aisle for prayer. I continued to watch as two team members prayed with her. She had severe arthritis. Her red swollen fingers protruded through leather supports and her hands were twisted and looked sore. To my astonishment her fingers returned to normal as I watched and she started to move her arms and hands. Then I noticed that her knees and ankles were also swollen. I watched to see if they would also return to normal, but nothing happened.

That evening I was having a late supper at the vicarage when the telephone rang. It was Nicola, the lady I had watched, who was now bubbling over with excitement. Because of her condition she had formerly been unable to brush her hair or even hold her new baby. Between tears and laughter she described how she could now hold the baby with one hand and brush her hair with the other. Naturally, I was delighted yet I was mystified as to why the Lord had not completed the healing.

Two weeks after we had returned home I was sitting quietly before the Lord when He reminded me of this event. He showed me that the real cause of this condition was a series of traumatic occurrences during her childhood which she was pushing down into the lower part of her body. Taking courage in both hands I telephoned the vicar's wife and arranged to travel down the next day.

We rang the doorbell and I heard Nicola shuffling up the hallway to let us in. She looked radiant, and was moving the upper half of her body freely. I told her what I believed was the cause of her illness. She said that my diagnosis could not be correct as her childhood, although at times difficult, had no traumatic ingredients such as I had inferred. However, she indicated that she would like more prayers. The powerful healing already received had raised her hopes.

We welcomed the Holy Spirit to continue the healing ministry of Jesus within her body. In the quietness that followed I had a word of knowledge to the effect that the cause of the illness related to her mother. She initially said that her relationship with her mother was fine, but then she started to weep.

Through her tears she told me her story. Her father had left her mother when she was twelve, and had had a number of inconclusive relationships. Simultaneously, her mother found that her twelve-year-old daughter was becoming a nuisance and needed more supervision. Not wanting to alter her own way of life, she tried to hand over her parental responsibility to Nicola's grandmother. Nicola arrived home one day in the middle of a terrible argument. Her mother and grandmother were yelling at each other in the lounge. As she listened it became apparent that she was actually the cause of it. Her mother didn't want her but her elderly grandmother felt that she couldn't cope with the responsibility. As she stood looking through the open door, she suddenly saw her mother attempt to strangle her grandmother. The trauma of this incident was manifesting itself in a crippling disease.

As I counselled and prayed I encouraged Nicola to focus on this painful event, and then to forgive her mother and bless her. This took her some time to do, but she was finally able to forgive her. We then prayed for the Holy Spirit to come upon her, and a burning heat began to affect every joint of her body. This sensation lasted for about twenty minutes and then the heat left her body as suddenly as it had come. She had been seated while we were praying and I took her hand and drew her to her feet. The swellings in the joints had almost disappeared and all the pain had gone. She was surprised and I was overwhelmed by the goodness of God. During the drive home I spent the time praising the Lord for such a wonderful healing.

Wherever we travelled during the next few months I gave her healing as a testimony to the power of God. Then something happened which put us back to square one. Arriving home from a trip, Mary told me that Nicola had telephoned and was very upset. When I made contact she explained that after two months in the clear her arthritis had returned. She told me in tears that her condition was almost as bad as before we prayed the first time. I was stunned and decided to re-route a weekend away with Mary so that we could visit her. What she proceeded to tell us was illuminating.

Her ageing mother now longed for the loving close mother/ daughter relationship which they had never had. To achieve this the mother was using emotional blackmail, and making demands which were unacceptable. As Nicola had lain awake one night going over this intolerable situation, her arthritic condition suddenly returned. I sought to explain to her that the guilt she was experiencing was entirely false and in my prayer I broke its power in the name of Jesus.

When Mary and I prayed for her, the healing came back once more to her body. Her husband was with us and I suggested that if there should be any recurrence then he should minister to her as we had done. Subsequently we heard that the healing had stabilised.

I have also noticed that traumatic events outside the family situation can equally damage emotions and result in physical problems. Belinda came from a happy caring family. I was asked if I could see her after she had come down from university where she had failed three of her second year examinations. As she had revised for the examinations a tension had built up within her, and on the morning of the third examination she had developed a blind panic from which she still had not recovered.

That was the background, but the main reason I had been asked to see her was to pray for her eyesight which had deteriorated badly over the years. As the Holy Spirit came upon her she began to experience a series of sensations. Firstly, a pressure built up in her head and then a band of heat flitted across her brow and eyes. At first her eyes began to flutter but then became tightly closed in a way that she was unable to control. While this was happening she felt God was doing something for her sight. However, within minutes a large shutter suddenly seemed to come down and cut her off from the presence of God.

We sat and talked and I sensed that, underlying her problems, was a past hurt which was crippling her personality. Casting her mind back on the early years of childhood, she could remember nothing which could be regarded as 'traumatic'.

The following Sunday afternoon she was telling her father what had happened and said how puzzled she was about my suggestion of some past hurt. Her father then told her of an incident when, as a two-year-old, she had been taken to a strict Scottish hospital to have a squint in the eye corrected. She was admitted to an adult ward which only allowed visiting at stated hours. On the morning of the operation her father had arrived to find his daughter screaming with terror in the presence of a white clad and masked orderly. Her father was allowed to carry her to the operating theatre, but at the swing doors she was handed back to the orderly who placed her on the operating table. Even as her father told this story she began to panic. The healing of this trauma put an end to years of irrational behaviour and physical afflictions.

Often when sharing our faith we find it difficult to know where to begin. People today, although they have feelings of guilt, are seldom aware that they have sinned against God and need to seek forgiveness through Christ. In certain instances I have found it easier to talk about how Jesus heals an inward problem without ever mentioning that it is the result of sin. It is to this awareness of need that the gospel can be applied.

Andrew and Penny invited Mary and me to speak at a supper party which they had organised for neighbours and friends, a number of whom were practising Christians. On arrival we found their Hampstead flat crowded to overflowing. Late in the evening Andrew introduced me officially and said that I would talk about what I had seen God doing during a recent trip.

The evening was warm and wine had flowed liberally, so I was not surprised when at least two guests nodded off while I was speaking! To those who were listening I simply shared instances in which we had seen the Holy Spirit in action. I spoke of a well-known Irish folk singer who, because of his work, had arrived late at a meeting at which one of our team was ministering. He asked me if I would pray for a fear that had persistently troubled him from childhood. In his own words, it always took the joy from his life.

Whilst praying I perceived that he had been confined in a dark space as a little boy. I mentioned this and in his endearing Irish accent he recounted such an incident which had happened to him. He had been playing in a disused furnace and someone had shut the door and locked it. Some hours were to pass before distraught parents found him. In his mind he saw himself again in the furnace and the feelings of panic and fear welled up within. We asked the Holy Spirit to release this trapped emotion of fear and a sense of freedom and peace came upon him.

I cited instances of people who had experienced physical healings and others who had come to know Christ. After fifteen minutes I invited questions. Then Andrew suddenly earthed what had been shared. He wanted to know if the Holy Spirit would actually come at that moment and work among us if we asked Him. I assured him that He would indeed, and so Andrew asked me to pray.

The Holy Spirit fell upon a number of people that night and I asked if anyone would like prayer for healing. A Jewess named Sarah got up and came to the centre of the lounge. She was suffering from a painful physical problem. In Jesus' name we prayed and immediately she felt her body being filled with a powerful heat which was to last for thirty or more minutes. As I sought the Lord I perceived that her physical condition was just a symptom of deep inner turmoils and hurts. In my mind I could see the Holocaust – Jewish refugees moving from place to place, persecuted and rejected. It was as if behind her there was a great wave hovering, always ready to break and engulf her. While I related this to her, she kept nodding.

In Sarah's life there was still much for the Lord to unravel, but a journey had begun. During a conversation later I told her that Jesus had said that He would baptise with the Holy Spirit and fire, and that was what she had just experienced. She said she had not practised her faith for some years, but had recently begun to seek God again. Through Andrew and Penny she had heard about Jesus and now, by God's grace, this daughter of Abraham was experiencing something of His love in her life. However, although we knew what was happening, she had trouble relating her experience to Jesus.

Seven months later I was surprised to see Sarah at St Andrew's. I noticed during the service that she had both hands raised in worship, and wondered what had transpired since our last meeting.

At the end of the service she asked for prayer. She said that that evening she had experienced the presence of God as on the previous occasion. Again I told her it was the Spirit of Jesus who was seeking to come into her life. This time she reacted with hostility and said she wished I wouldn't talk about Jesus in such terms.

Later that week she made an appointment to see me. During our conversation she told me the story of her life, which involved much suffering, and accounted for much of her present insecurity and fear. I then shared something of my own experiences and described how Jesus had come to me and started a healing of my personality which was still going on. We then talked at great length before Sarah asked me simply to tell her how she could know Jesus.

To me it was obvious that Jesus was already involved in her life, and that what she needed was to acknowledge that fact and positively welcome Him. I suggested we pray together.

As I asked the Holy Spirit to come and reveal Jesus to her, Sarah had a picture of a cross. On it she saw a figure suffering agonising pain. I told her it was Jesus dying in order that she might be forgiven. The second picture she saw was of Jesus standing facing her with outstretched arms. I suggested this was the living Jesus welcoming her. She told me that as she responded she was surrounded by a dazzling light. Within minutes she was praising Him in an unknown tongue.

In similar experiences to those described I have known the relief which comes when deep hurts are brought to the surface and are met by the healing power of Jesus. However, though for the first week one may feel as if life has been completely changed, sometimes there may be a slipping back into the old destructive thought patterns and there is the temptation to wonder whether one had received any healing at all.

A bit of domestic DIY has often helped me to illustrate what may happen following any liberating experience of God in one's life. Our bedroom door had warped and, as a result, would only open half way. For eighteen months there were always more pressing jobs to be done and we grew accustomed to this limitation. But eventually I took the door down and planed nearly half an inch off the bottom. The difference was immediate, although at first it seemed rather strange. However, although I now knew the door would open fully, I still occasionally found myself reverting to my former practice, involuntarily pushing the door only half way. Gradually the new attitude replaced the old and the episode was forgotten. Some six months after this household repair job, I was rushing into the bedroom to change my shoes. Suddenly I stopped in my tracks, amazed at myself. For some unknown reason I had only opened the door half way – the old practice once again.

In my own life I became aware that, under pressure, the old feelings of insecurity returned and I had to learn to discard these from my mind. It became a matter of simple discipline.

My initial experience of inner healing unearthed other buried emotions. I have always been a good sleeper and once my head touches the pillow I usually know nothing more until the alarm breaks the peace. For no apparent reason I suddenly started to wake up in the night, absolutely terrified. I felt that there was a man in the room and he was walking towards me. For many months this was at least a twice weekly experience. One day I was sharing this with a friend and asked him if he would pray for me.

As he prayed my memory recalled a time when I was about twelve years old. We were all on a holiday in Christchurch, New Zealand. I had woken up to see a man standing in the doorway of my bedroom. In the half light he started to tiptoe to the foot of my bed. Thinking it was my father, I spoke to him, whereupon he moved quietly out of the room. Petrified, I froze in my bed until I had enough courage to run to my parents' room and tell them what I thought had happened.

I told John what I had experienced and he asked Jesus to free me from the memory. My immediate feelings were of release and peace, but I wondered how it would affect my sleep pattern. I needn't have wondered – that experience has never returned.

One very helpful thing I heard John Wimber say when he first visited us was that 'my brother is my brother and my enemy is the devil'. He was making the point that we often think of fellow Christians who disagree with us as our enemies when they are in fact our brothers. We only have one enemy and that is the devil who, as Jesus told us, came to kill and destroy. Every mention of his activities in the Gospels bears this out. When Satan sees a weakness he attacks it and traumatic events leave wounds in our lives which make us vulnerable to Satan.

In some instances an evil presence may attach itself to the trauma, though it would be quite wrong to assume this about every past emotional hurt. A woman of forty-five, for whom we were praying, started to cry. This was particularly significant. The last time she had cried was as a six-year-old when she had been appallingly violated by her father. We discerned that in this case a demon had entered her life at that point. As I commanded the evil spirit to depart in Jesus' name she experienced a sense of strangulation. Her head moved involuntarily from side to side and her face became grotesque. Then she told us that she sensed something had left her and her whole body became as relaxed as jelly.

I have only seen this happen with a small number of people. In such cases I have found that afterwards the enemy seeks to pound the sensitive, emotional areas with the feelings that once held the sufferer captive. On such occasions I encourage people to resist him, even commanding him audibly in the name of Jesus to go to the place where he belongs. The Scriptures say, 'Resist the devil, and he will flee from you' (James 4:7). If he continues to harass I suggest further prayer with a minister.

I find the travelling ministry emotionally very draining. On an average team visit I lead five evening meetings, based on homes. These can last up to five hours and involve continuous dialogue with unbelievers. During the day there may be a three-hour team meeting, and in the afternoon either more groups or personal counselling. At the weekends I preach at the services and also at the public meetings for the area, which are usually held in a civic centre or theatre. Besides this, I pray with dozens of people and support the team, who also have similar strains.

When I arrive home Mary, who has borne all the responsibilities of our family and home, naturally wants to hand them back to me. Within hours of returning there are family decisions to take; repair men to contact; urgent calls to make regarding future ministries; lawns to mow; and a response to make to the inevitable criticisms on some area of our ministry.

In the early days Mary and I found this a strain on our relationship. Whilst away I looked forward so much to being with her and the family, but when I arrived home I was hardly able to cope. Sometimes I would weep, and old patterns of insecurity and fear would re-emerge. On such occasions I would decide to resign and apply to be a minister of a small country parish. However, with the passing of time, Mary realised more than I what was happening. She counselled me to be gentle with myself and allow time for my emotions to be renewed. But this was easier said than done.

When a church invites a team to visit them or their town, they have certain expectations. These are all spiritual. They are hoping that neighbours and friends will become Christians. A number are looking to the team for counsel, others are believing that the Holy Spirit will be poured out at the meetings, and people will be healed and renewed. As a result we find for ten days we are intensely involved in spiritual activity.

On returning home I find prayer, Bible reading and worship are the last things I want to do. I feel as if I don't want to attend another home group, pray with another person, or preach one more sermon ever again. However, the real problem is emotional exhaustion, and I find that only time and a change of activity will heal this.

For many of us the healing of emotional hurts has made us

want to share our faith with others. It has given us a testimony to the power and reality of Jesus. Until that time we worshipped, prayed, and believed, but there was something in our lives which was more powerful than the new life which Jesus had given. In my own instance I lived my life out of feelings of rejection and insecurity. It was not until the force of these was broken that I discovered the power of Jesus and His resurrection. Out of this came a travelling ministry.

Chapter 7

AVAILABLE – WILL TRAVEL

We were driving down the A20 in order to take a weekend for a church in Surrey. Liz was sitting with me in the front of the car and we were reminiscing with the others in the car about the ways in which the Faith Sharing Ministry had changed since we had first started twelve years earlier. Liz described it this way: 'In the past our team supplied the action through teaching, testimony, drama, dance and music. Now God is supplying His own drama.' It is exciting to look back and see how God has changed us.

The spring of 1974 found our church at the crossroads. Much had happened in the life of the fellowship and we realised that, unless we could give away what we had received from God, then it would eventually stagnate and die. I was spending a few days in the New Forest when God spoke to me. He began to show me the implications of Jesus' command to the church to wait for the Holy Spirit's power, and then go with the gospel into the locality, the nation and the world (Acts 1:4–8).

I returned home with the over-riding feeling that we as a church should go where Jesus indicated. Reading the Gospels and the Acts of the Apostles afresh, I noticed that the gospel pioneers usually travelled in teams. It occurred to me that they were like faith sharing teams; just ordinary people who were able to share what God had done in Jesus' name, and what His Spirit was doing in them both individually and corporately. As I have shown in chapter 1, our church

immediately took up the idea and soon set me free to direct
and develop it.

From my reading of Acts it seemed to me that mission
was always initiated by the Holy Spirit. I decided that we
would never suggest to anyone that we should visit their
church; we would always wait for invitations. This was
difficult to begin with, and was the cause of a number of
humorous incidents. In the early stages a vicar telephoned
me from Doncaster to enquire about the possibility of a team
visit in eighteen months' time. I replied that actually we
could even manage the following weekend. However, we
waited and our diary gradually began to fill up.

When an invitation arrived I would first encourage the
vicar or staff of the church to visit me in Chorleywood for a
working lunch. At this meeting my colleague, Iain Roberts,
and I would try and build up a picture of the type of parish
and its particular needs. Today we send the church leaders
back with a video which demonstrates something of our
ministry and we request that it be shown to the Parochial
Church Council, or whatever group is considering the possibility of a Faith Sharing visit. If they want to pursue the idea,
then we return the visit. We make it clear at this meeting
that we shall only come if a representative group still wants
us. By inviting us, this group will also be committing
itself to be involved in whatever we may be led to do.
After these consultations I then decide about the right
time and the right team to go. This procedure is vitally
important.

Besides those who are helped in their faith, there are others
who will react negatively. Before I had implemented this
procedure we went to a number of churches which operated
as a team. Unknown to me, on one occasion one team leader
had great reservations about our visit and type of ministry
which didn't surface until after we had left. Instead of leading
the churches on, he sided with those having difficulty, and
wrote in a widely circulated magazine that he questioned
whether our ministry was really Christian. Whenever a team
ministers in the power of the Spirit, there will be opposition

and difficulties. For this reason the inviting leadership must be fully behind the insights we seek to share.

People often ask me about the financing of this ministry. St Andrew's pays my salary and provides accommodation as part of its missionary giving. The church takes all forms of missionary giving seriously and, without putting itself under law about it, seeks to give at least half of the total budget to mission. We invite any church we visit to pay the petrol for our cars, and to make a gift towards the Faith Sharing Ministry.

It is our policy that finance must not dictate ministry and if we feel that a particular invitation is a call from God, then we accept it. This means that we may send three cars to an inner city church in the north of England and only receive a token gift. However, we find that at the end of each year the gifts from the wealthier churches subsidise the poorer.

Two weeks before a team travels for a Faith Sharing weekend, it meets with its leader. The team will comprise between eight and ten people. I have a nucleus of three who always travel with me. They are Iain and Joan Roberts and Shirley Hartup. Shirley leads my team's worship while Iain shares the teaching with me. To join this nucleus I invite two couples and a single person, three of whom have probably not travelled with a team before.

Qualifications for such a team are simple. Each member must have a relationship with Jesus which he can confidently and humbly talk about. He must be open to receive ministry and also to be able to minister. This is one of the areas in which David and I complement each other. Once a month, on a Saturday morning, David teaches on 'ministering in the power of the Spirit' and team members attend this.

A team member needs to be fully committed and involved in what is happening at St Andrew's. There is nothing more destructive than a person who talks critically about his church and its leaders. This doesn't mean that our difficulties are pushed under the carpet – rather, the reverse is true. I encourage openness about our individual failings and those of our church. We find that during a team visit a number of local people will take the opportunity of sharing problems with us. Often they start the conversation by saying they have never shared the particular problem with anyone before, not even their wife or husband. Sometimes it is to do with having committed adultery, or feeling guilty because of an abortion. The problem could be incest or physical abuse suffered as a child. We must receive the disclosure without being judgmental, and be able to keep it strictly confidential. At times we find ourselves in situations where people are being critical of their leaders. Our presence as outsiders provides the opportunity for some to comment on everything they disagree with in the life of their church. We seek to give wholehearted support to all that the vicar is doing.

A preparation meeting is held for the team at which the group will be told about the leadership and people in the parish to be visited. The team leader will have spoken recently to the vicar, who will have brought him up to date on what is happening in the fellowship. The rest of the evening is spent in worship and listening to God. As we wait upon the Lord, usually a theme begins to emerge. This will come from scripture passages, prophecy and pictures. We often find that the message has quite startling results in the church we go to. On one occasion the theme revolved around a passage from the Song of Solomon, where the Lord comes to woo the girl who is hiding under the stairs. It transpired that a number of people in this particular church had been reading this very passage the week before our visit. They felt that they were like the girl in question and that the Lord was calling them to leave the 'dark and fearful place' and go to Him. It was clearly more than a coincidence when a team member read the passage as he introduced the theme. One of the people present broke down in tears.

On these Faith Sharing weekends we have travelled to over 250 churches, as far afield as Truro in the west, Leeds in the north, and Norwich in the east. Sometimes we arrive as late as midnight on the Friday evening, to be met and taken to our respective hosts. We find that living with a family is one of the valuable aspects of the weekend. The vicar will sometimes ask people on the fringe of his congregation to be our hosts and as often as not the couple will have been led to some further commitment to Jesus Christ by the time we leave on the Sunday evening. There are light, as well as serious moments.

Frank and Tony, two of our team, are very different. Tony is a brilliant musician. When he joined our team he had only just become a Christian, having come from an occult background. He had long hair, old worn jeans and sweat shirt. When the weather turned cold he wrapped himself in a greasy duffle coat! Frank was then Clerk of the Journals at the House of Commons, a much respected figure, who on two occasions had been acknowledged in the Honours List. Frank and Tony duly arrived late one Friday evening, and were met at the vicarage by a widow who was to be their hostess for the weekend. Being tired they wanted to go straight to bed. Their hostess showed them to the bedroom in which was a small double bed!

Val and Liz were also being shown to their bedroom when their hostess handed them a glass of water each. The girls replied that they didn't usually take water to bed whereupon the hostess asked them what they would do with their teeth!

Arriving in a village community in the depths of winter, I stayed on a farm. It was difficult getting to the farmhouse as snow had fallen. However, we eventually slithered up the farm track, to be greeted by the farmer in a short-sleeved summer shirt! I was taken into the kitchen where an ancient Raeburn stove did its best to melt the ice on the windows. My host and hostess were delightful and led me up an antiquated stairway to my bedroom. As I climbed higher I became vividly aware that there was no heating at all in the house.

From my bedroom window I was shown an incredible view, made even more beautiful by a winter sun glistening on fresh snow. When they left me to unpack I looked at my bed. To my consternation it was covered by a nylon sheet and one blanket. That evening I dressed for bed – I put on all the clothes I had, plus a scarf and duffel coat with hood. I declined a cup of tea in bed in the morning on the pretext that it might disturb my spiritual meditations.

Another interesting week was spent in a northern parish. Mary and I stayed in the home of a young married couple who had a baby a few months old. Their flat was tiny and whilst they slept on the settee in the lounge we had their double bed – and the baby. Bottles were left ready to be heated and during the night Mary would feed the child. This arrangement lasted three nights. On the fourth, the baby had breathing difficulties and was rushed into hospital.

The Saturday morning programme of a Faith Sharing weekend begins with a session entitled 'Open to God'. This is just what it implies – an opportunity through scripture meditation, gently led worship, and silence to hear God and to respond to Him in confession, thanksgiving, and praise. For many people, caught up with the hurry, worry, noise and tension surrounding their everyday lives, this introduction can be strangely threatening. In some instances when the quiet has stretched out for ten minutes or so, people have got up and left the room. When I have spoken with them later they have confessed that they couldn't cope with so much silence. It makes some feel vulnerable and fearful. For others it may even create panic.

But I have also had many letters from people who found this opening time the highlight of our visit. Frank, for example, wrote that it was during the silence that he had what he could only describe as a deep experience of the peace and reality of God. June, in great detail, described how she started to weep as in the silence the Lord came to her and took away all the anxieties and fears which had always dominated her life.

Sometimes we are invited into parishes where the vicar may have been inducted only a few months previously. He has probably inherited a run down congregation of around thirty or forty, the majority of whom believe in God but have little concept of a personal relationship with Jesus Christ. In such circumstances our second session comprises teaching on what commitment to Jesus means. This is supported by testimonies from the team members.

From the outset I realised how powerful personal testimony can be. On one occasion I had Ken and Jeanne in the teams. Ken is a partner in a firm of accountants. He lives in a large house with swimming pool and games room. He began by telling the conference that up to a few years previously God had played no part in their lives at all. Then one day tragedy struck. Their little girl was drowned in the swimming pool. He recounted the subsequent events which included his anger at a member of our staff who rushed to the hospital to be with them.

Jeanne picked up their story and related how this event had led to her seeking God. She told how each time she went to St Andrew's she cried through the whole service. At the end she went for prayer and the laying-on-of-hands, and discovered over a period of time that her grief lessened and she came to know Jesus, her comforter and friend, as her Lord and Saviour.

Ken continued their testimony and told us that while this was happening to Jeanne he was shutting his life off from God by immersing himself in his work. He had attended two meetings which Mary and I had in our house for those on the fringe of faith. After the second meeting he said that he would not be returning because what he had heard was completely irrelevant to his life and needs.

Because of Jeanne's involvement with St Andrew's Ken found himself with a set of new friends who persuaded him to go to church with them to hear Canon Keith de Berry, a retired rector of St Aldates, Oxford, now turned evangelist. Keith gave one illustration which was to lead Ken to Jesus. He asked the congregation what they thought they would find at the centre of an onion, after all the shells had been stripped away. At the end of a long silence Ken had said, 'Nothing.' He then asked what would be found at the centre of our lives if our money, job, material goods and family were all taken away. Ken realised that there would be nothing and, as Keith pointed the congregation to Jesus, Ken received Him.

When Ken and Jeanne had finished there was hardly a dry eye in the place. People then asked them questions about the difference knowing Christ had meant to them. Jeanne replied first and said that her experience had given her a concern for women who lose children through miscarriage, cot death or accident. She had founded a local organisation to help care for such people.

Ken said that he had always seen life in terms of success and money, but now he realised that people were much more important. He described how he had bought a coach and converted it into a coffee bar in order to create a meeting place for young people who find it difficult to relate with the church and had nowhere to go in the evenings. With Christian friends he manned this three nights a week, sharing with the young people the joy of knowing Jesus.

Another team member who had come to a living faith in Christ from a more traditional background also gave a testimony. As a result many people in that church committed their lives to Christ during the conference.

I receive letters from vicars of established congregations who write that they are like the disciples in the Ephesian church who had never heard that there was a Holy Spirit. With such churches we start with teaching about the person of the Holy Spirit. This is based on what Jesus said about Him and the experiences that were to be expected when He came. Again, team testimony forms an important part of the sharing.

On Saturday afternoons we usually have a number of seminars. Team members are not specialists but they do act as catalysts. A vicar writing to thank me for a Faith Sharing weekend said that he didn't believe that we had said anything new, but real help had come through allowing his people to talk about what they felt and believed. He also felt that our prayer ministry at the end of the services had enabled many to receive what they had been searching for.

I have known times in the type of church I first mentioned

when nearly half of the conference would attend a seminar on 'Becoming a Christian'. This is a form where doubts can be aired and simple questions asked without embarrassment. I never cease to be surprised at the answers I get to the question, 'If God was to meet you at heaven's gate and ask you why you thought He should let you in, what reason would you give?' The majority say it is because of the decent life they have lived. Such replies give the team an opportunity to talk about the grace of God and the significance of the death and resurrection of Jesus.

An equally popular seminar deals with the work of the Holy Spirit. Among other things, the leader teaches about the Holy Spirit's gifts and ministries, and illustrations are given from the team members' experiences. It was whilst leading this seminar in 1978 that God made me aware of a credibility gap which existed between what I was teaching and what the group actually experienced. In my introduction I spoke of the four metaphors of fire, wind, oil and water as descriptions of the Holy Spirit's action, taking my illustrations from the portions of scripture where these occurred. After a discussion I went for tea with a young man who said to me very candidly, 'So what?' He went on to say that he had never experienced the Holy Spirit in any of the ways I had mentioned, and to his knowledge neither had any of his contemporaries in his church or university. As if to add insult to injury, he asked me what experience I had had of the Holy Spirit working in the ways which I had taught and illustrated. Taking a deep breath, I admitted 'very little'. This was a dimension that we were soon going to learn a lot more about.

In these seminars, where there needs to be a lot of inter-relating, we have developed a method of leading discussions after the introductory talk. For some seminars we divide up into two or even three groups of about twelve people. The groups sit in a circle and the leader encourages each member to introduce himself. He then reverses the order and asks if each person would like to share something that had been meaningful to him in the introduction. We find that once everyone has spoken twice in the group then the rest of the discussion is inclined to go fairly easily. Sometimes we have found it helpful to discuss a number of questions based upon a set scriptural passage. On other occasions the group has raised questions during the initial sharing and the time is used profitably in discussing them.

My closest colleague in the Faith Sharing Ministry during the last eleven years is a retired consultant neuro-surgeon, Iain Roberts. He and a small team lead a seminar on 'inner healing'. This is particularly valuable where the Holy Spirit has already been working new things. In such churches people will say to me: 'I just don't know what is happening to me. My vicar prayed over me that I might know the power of the Holy Spirit, and instead of joy I am feeling hurt and fearful.' Iain and the team seek to help such people to see how the Holy Spirit brings up many past hurts which we have all spent a lifetime keeping down. This may cause us to feel some painful emotion, which is the last thing most of us want. But what is kept in the dark belongs to the enemy – what is brought to the light the Holy Spirit can heal.

In the worship seminar those leading seek to explore the whole area of creative worship. Those who attend are in either a choir or an ad hoc music group. Our leader explores the scriptural principles involved in leading worship and the group is encouraged to compose a hymn with a musical setting. Running parallel with the music workshop may be one for those gifted in sacred dance or drama. In some situations the Saturday evening will consist of a celebration where what has been prepared in these groups will be shared with the congregation.

We have always thought of evangelism in terms of simply sharing our faith with those who don't have any. A seminar on this subject is particularly popular where people have come alive in the Spirit and want to share their faith in Jesus with friends and neighbours. Our method has always been through homes. Any who might be interested are invited by Christian friends to meet members of our team; there are usually two from the team in each group. The leader will begin the evening with a five minute presentation of the gospel and this is followed by an up-to-date testimony from another team member about the reality of Jesus in daily life. During this seminar we mention the type of questions which have usually been raised at the hundreds of such meetings which our teams have now led. We always stress that we have no glib answers for many major problems in life, but we have Jesus who stands beside all the unanswerable questions as One who has suffered and, through His death and resurrection, has triumphed over the ultimate unanswerable question, 'My God, why have you forsaken me?'

The teaching methods of Jesus are quite simple. He first taught His disciples that He wanted them to go out with the good news of the kingdom of God and heal the sick. Next He showed them how to do it. Then He sent them out in twos to do it. I have sought to adopt this principle, so that at the Saturday evening outreach meeting our team members take with them a couple from the local fellowship, in order to let them put into practice what they have learned at the earlier sessions on the Saturday.

For many this is their first opportunity to witness and speak of Jesus. Many have been encouraged at the end of the evening to hear a neighbour asking how he could know Christ. Such a request has been the opportunity to pray with a seeker. During a Faith Sharing visit to Canford Magna parish church so many meetings had been organised that our team members could not be involved in all of them. One local man, who had never led such a meeting, did so and was overjoyed at the end when a visitor asked if he would pray with him to receive Christ.

We see the Sunday services as opportunities for the congregation to respond to the teaching and testimony which they have heard the previous day. In many churches this is the first time such an opportunity has been given. In a large evangelical church in the south of England I gave such an invitation at the end of the evening service. I had arranged with the vicar that I would close the service and pronounce the blessing. I gave explicit instructions that after the blessing all who needed to go would be free to leave and those who would like to respond to the message with personal prayer could wait behind. Imagine my surprise when nearly the whole congregation of three hundred or more stayed seated. Thinking that they had not understood my instructions, I repeated them. After five minutes I realised that all wanted prayer and suggested they come forward as if for Communion. It was nearly eleven o'clock before our team left the building that night.

Such weekends can be used by the leadership of a church in a variety of ways. Obviously it can be a reaping time when those with evangelistic gifts can bring seekers into the kingdom of God. In some churches we find that the vicar and a group of lay people have come into renewal and the rest of the congregation is either strongly disapproving or simply bewildered by what is happening. A team coming from outside can show that what is happening in their church is quite normal and good. Again it can be an affirming experience for those who have already been renewed.

Many leaders use such weekends as a launching pad. For six months they may have taught about the type of fellowship encountered in the early church. This was the experience of John Simons, vicar of Holy Trinity, Nailsea. He had chosen and trained leaders intending, after our visit, to start regular home meetings within the parish. Others have established a regular healing ministry or introduced a time of open worship in their services where an opportunity can be given for spontaneous prayer or prophecy.

When I first meet the church leadership to plan a Faith Sharing team visit I stress that it is important to be prepared to give away what they receive. At St Luke's, Cranham, after our visit the curate, John Reeves, was appointed to lead similar teams in the diocese of Cheltenham. When John became vicar another full time appointment was made, and Charlie Cleaverly led the 'Together Teams'. Following a prophetic word while visiting St Luke's, Hackney, the then vicar, Charles May, also started to travel regularly with teams to many parts of the country. Following our visits numerous churches have gone out to share what they had received with others.

The benefits to the sending church cannot be overestimated. I have involved over two hundred of our congregation in this ministry and the blessings to St Andrew's have been enormous. Many of our people have experienced God working through them and in many instances have led other people to Christ, or prayed and seen them healed. On returning from such visits our people are able to share what God has done but, more than that, they have a new testimony. Often whilst commuting to London or queueing in the supermarket a neighbour or acquaintance will ask what they were doing the previous weekend. It is an opportunity for sharing faith in a fresh and natural way – just telling what God has done!

Such a ministry gives a church a wider and therefore more balanced view of the body of Christ – they are not limited by their often insular situation. We find that when the Holy Spirit begins to work in a new way there are two main reactions. Some believe that the church should respond more fully to what God is doing, whilst others feel that the changes are too radical and need to be slowed down. People from either group can find it very enlightening to go on a team. One of those who was frustrated by what they termed our slowness said, after being with a team to Somerset, that she was so thankful for what God had done at St Andrew's. She had seen that we had really taken a big leap forward. Others on a similar trip subsequently said that they now realised how important it was for the church to go on in the Holy Spirit. A faith sharing team is also a learning team. The name implies a sharing of faith, and privately and in groups this is what our teams do.

However, there are so many ways in which we learn from the life of the congregation to which we go. My vision has always been that such teams should eventually be led by lay people. With this in mind a few years ago I began to share the leadership with a number of men until I was able to let them lead the weekends. I now seek to introduce this policy to churches we are intending to visit. For many this is a new idea. They do not think it is proper for a team to come without a minister or priest in charge. However, we are gradually breaking this prejudice down and now five lay leaders regularly take teams in response to invitations.

Another aspect of this ministry is the offering of continuous support to struggling congregations in much more difficult situations than we find ourselves. When Graham Pulkingham first came to England with the Fisherfolk we were one of the first parishes they visited. We felt that they had so much to teach us and we invited them for weekends to our church and also for a houseparty, which was a watershed in our church life. Graham met with our leadership and groups visited them in their community near Reading. We likewise have sought, after an initial visit to an inner city church, to maintain links and provide support.

All these things we used to do – and still do – and God has blessed what we have done. But the preparations for our Faith Sharing Ministry always seemed like very hard work. Plays and dances had to be rehearsed and talks and testimonies thoroughly written. A programme was given to each member showing where their contribution fitted in and the time allocated for it. As the weekend approached I was always slightly anxious that we might not end it properly or someone would forget their lines. I planned for God to have His opportunity to do anything He wanted during a time following the morning and evening services. I was also aware that, although people were being helped, there was a lack of spiritual power in the ministry.

When John Wimber visited our church in 1981 I realised instantly what had been the missing dimension in the Faith Sharing Ministry. In many respects John's approach was little different from what we had been seeking to do during the previous seven years. However, there was one notable difference. He simply allowed the Holy Spirit opportunity to work whenever, wherever, and however He wanted. John was obviously open to God for any revelation as to what He might want to do next in the congregation. We have tried to learn from this and to incorporate it into our Faith Sharing weekends and our 'God in Action' programmes. We make a point now of consciously seeking to listen to God and the results have proved very profitable and quite remarkable. However, it also meant a new direction in my own life which initially proved quite puzzling.

Chapter 8

TRYING TO HEAR GOD

I greatly appreciated the annual meetings I had with Robert Runcie, who was then Bishop of St Albans. I had gone to the first meeting with a certain amount of trepidation. Having, as I believed, a call to start the Faith Sharing Ministry, which had also been affirmed by St Andrew's Church, it was Bishop Robert who would have to license me. The problem was that he had just issued a circular to all the diocese saying how he expected to see the Sheffield Report implemented. This meant that no church within our deanery was, in the future, to have a curate and in the long term certain parishes would be amalgamated. My call was a challenge. I was asking him to make an exception and reverse the process.

During our meeting two things happened which have since affected my life radically. The first obviously concerned my ministry. He listened as I outlined what I hoped to do and then asked some very searching questions. After we had discussed the practical issues, he said he felt God was in the call and he would be happy to license me. We then went into his chapel where he prayed for me, asking the Lord to lead and guide me by His Holy Spirit. Every year subsequently he used to invite me to St Albans to give him an up-to-date report on the ministry. Before one such meeting I was shown into his study and, because of a telephone call, I had to wait for ten minutes before I could see him. On his glass coffee table was a book called *The Russian Mystics*.*

---

* *The Russian Mystics* by Sergius Bolshakoff (Mowbray, 1977).

It looked fascinating and I made a note to order a copy.

As soon as my copy arrived I began to read it and encountered men who had apparently found what I had been searching for. They had come through the silence to know God in their hearts. Many spoke of putting their personalities into their hearts and worshipping God from that perspective. Others wrote of being caught up in the spirit as they prayed the Jesus Prayer from within their hearts. Although their vocabulary was mystical, and I could not identify with it from my own experience, I realised there was much untapped reality which was scriptural but not of our western culture. The writer of the Proverbs encourages the reader in these terms: 'More than all else, keep watch over your heart, since here are the well springs of life' (Proverbs 4:23, JB) – and it was Jesus who had so much to say about the heart. It was from the heart there flowed 'streams of living water' (John 7:38). I was beginning to see the link between seeking God and silence.

I was with a team in Nottingham. For this particular weekend the local Anglicans and Methodists had combined and on the warm Saturday afternoon those attending had been divided into small groups which were scattered around the lawns and gardens belonging to the Methodist Church. My mind was elsewhere. In the evening I was to speak at a 'Celebration' and then twice on the Sunday, including a combined service in the evening. I withdrew slightly from the group and began to finger through a folder in which I had a collection of sermons that covered almost every eventuality. I found myself entering into what seemed to be a dialogue with the Lord. It went something like this:

'Barry, what are you doing?'

'Just looking in my collection, Lord, for three appropriate talks.'

There followed a pause as I thumbed through the collection again before withdrawing three possibles.

'Why have you chosen those in your hand?'

'I've been preaching these for four years and God has used them.'

'Barry, my son, you are dry. You need a regular retreat to be with Me.'

'But, Lord, I read my Bible and pray to You.'

'Yes, but you're frightened of silence and of listening to Me. You're becoming a professional talker about Me.'

This experience followed my reading of *The Russian Mystics* and so, on arriving home, I made enquiries as to where I could spend one day a week listening to the Lord. A friend suggested The Grail at Pinner. I discovered that this belonged to a Roman Catholic community which was seeking, through conferences and publications, to encourage renewal of spiritual life within the Catholic Church.

Betty, the community leader, welcomed me warmly when I called. I explained my ministry and said that I would like a place each week where I could be alone to seek God. In the beautiful and wild grounds of the Centre are a number of 'poustinia', and she took me to show me over one.

Inside was a bare wooden table with a chair and a bed stretching along one wall. A candle was in a bottle and there was a small old-fashioned wash basin into which you poured your own water. The window was difficult to open as a number of climbing roses in full bloom restricted its movement. Outside, a row of poplar trees bordered the lawn on one side and a rose garden lay on the other.

In my diary for the following week I marked out a date and looked forward to my first day at the Grail with growing anticipation. Thursday dawned bright, and I walked eagerly down the winding path to the poustinia. I have drawn much inspiration in my life from such spiritual writers as Carlo Caretto, St John of the Cross, St Benedict, and the Russian holy men. These were all people who loved the desert and its solitude.

I remember that my watch said 8.30 a.m. when I first arrived. Before me stretched another eight hours in which I could give the Lord all my time and attention. The thought excited me. On the wooden table I placed my Jerusalem

Bible which I use for devotional reading. Besides this I laid a
notebook and two pens of different colours. These all seemed
rather important in a room so devoid of furniture. I settled
down and looked at my watch again. It was 8.35.

Shutting my eyes I began to pray to the Lord in tongues.
As a prayer gift I have exercised this most days of my life for
nearly eighteen years. After a relatively short period it always
leads me into an awareness of the presence of God. Next, I
thanked God for the opportunity of being with Him and for
the joy and privilege of finding such an idyllic place. I sought
to recall everything for which I was at that time particularly
thankful. My thoughts ranged from family, to friends, to the
church, even through to material possessions and of course
His grace in bringing me to faith in Jesus.

The following weekend we were going to be in Leeds, so I
began to intercede for the vicar and his wife, the church
leaders, our team, and the travel arrangements. Although we
were away, our church had a busy programme, so I recalled
all the proposed events and asked the Lord to bless them.
After family, friends and the sick, I was struggling, so I
prayed the Lord's Prayer. I looked at my watch. It was 9.15!

Outside, the flowers looked particularly beautiful in the
morning light. The birds sang, oblivious of my presence. A
little tit landed about a foot from me and busied himself on a
sprig of the yellow climbing rose. I opened my Bible at the
Psalms and read one and then I turned to a chapter of
Proverbs before finding my place in John's Gospel, at the
Scripture Union reading for the day. This is a pattern I have
always sought to follow. Just after I received Christ, I heard
Billy Graham on a radio broadcast speaking on the subject of
'Knowing God'. He said that each morning he read one of the
Psalms, followed by a chapter from the Book of Proverbs; the
Psalms taught him how to approach God and Proverbs how
to live his life. On that Thursday I again followed this
pattern. Looking at my watch I could see that it was 9.45 – I
had been in the poustinia for an hour and a quarter. If my
arithmetic was correct, there were six and three quarter
hours to go!

Leaving my garden cell I went into the main house to see if a cup of coffee was being served. Cook, in her warm pleasant way, told me it was usually served at 11.00, but I could re-heat some that had been left over from breakfast. As the gas flame brought the coffee to the boil, I began to wonder what I was going to do for the rest of the day. Pouring the coffee into a mug, I retraced my steps down the path and through the little wood back into my seclusion.

I drank the coffee and thought of Carlo Caretto – a little brother belonging to the Community of Charles de Fourcauld. Carlo spent six months of his year in a cave in the Sahara desert and the rest of the year working in a slum in one of the world's major cities. His writing gives the impression that in the quietness of the desert God was with him in powerful ways. It was there that he heard God, who gave the inner strength he needed to help the poor and downtrodden, and also the inspiration for his many books. By now the sun was streaming through the window – I sat back in my hard wooden chair and relaxed. It was exactly eleven o'clock when I awoke!

To clear my head I went for a walk. I passed the weaving hut where Ursula was busy at the loom making a carpet or wall hanging from wool which she had dyed and spun. Leaving the buildings behind, I walked out towards the orchard and the woods. For some reason God had apparently deserted me. I had faithfully done all the things which I had been taught to do, and now at 11.15 I was beginning to feel quite fed up. As I approached the woods I sensed the Lord saying to me: 'Barry, when are you going to be still and look to Me?'

Wandering back to the poustinia I sat down again. Immediately I found myself fighting the temptation to say something, or turn up a favourite passage of scripture, or go for another walk, or have a second cup of coffee. It was then that I decided, come what may, I was going to sit still for an hour. If God wanted to speak, I was ready to listen. At this point the battle really began. My mind started to rotate like a merry-go-round, filled with thoughts of impending commitments and responsibilities. I tried as best I could to put the brakes on and bring every thought to Christ. Slowly, ever so slowly, my mind slowed down and began to reflect the quietness of the surroundings.

Having begun to master my own thoughts, something more sinister started to happen. I suddenly felt fearful and wanted to leave the poustinia. It came to me that this solitude and stillness was something that specially dedicated people were able to endure and benefit from. I had been ordained for many years and except for the occasional retreat I had managed to maintain my spiritual life on regular morning devotions and prayers. I began to think that I had probably got the whole business out of proportion.

Fortunately I had decided to stay put for an hour and reluctantly I sat still and resisted the fear. It occurred to me that while Jesus was alone in the wilderness for forty days He also had a devilish visitation. The devil tried to undermine the relationship which Jesus had with the Father. I had only been alone for three and a half hours, but I realised that the devil was trying to make me fearful.

The devil threw into my mind fear of death and of the future and suggested many lustful fantasies. I had had these before on many occasions, but never so concentrated as then. In such circumstances, Paul counselled the Ephesian Christians to put up the shield of faith by which they could put out all these 'fiery darts of the evil one'. 'Fiery darts' is an apt description of such assaults. If a lighted arrow penetrated and pierced a building, it might easily cause the building to be engulfed in flames. If the devil's fiery darts are not quickly quenched they can destroy us and our work for God.

At last I was able to maintain the silence and waited patiently for the Lord to speak to me. I was intrigued about how this might actually happen. Only once have I ever heard God in an audible voice and that was just after arriving at St Andrew's. Mary and I, having spent four years in the sleepy West Country, found ourselves suddenly thrust into the crippling pace of suburbia. We were like fish out of water and overwhelmed by a full church and what, we felt, were their expectations of us. At my commissioning one of the leaders had given me a scripture from Deuteronomy about the Lord's promise of guidance. The next morning I went into my study and knelt by an old prayer desk. I felt bewildered. Hardly had I knelt when a voice in front of me said simply: 'I will direct you.' For me this has always been the Lord and a promise which I have often fallen back on in times of bewilderment.

It was now 2 p.m. – the hour was up – and yet God still hadn't spoken. I thought that I would give Him another half hour and then go home. During this final period I once again became very conscious of the time so I took my watch off and put it in my pocket. I could no longer hear its ticks – but neither could I hear God. I listened, but no audible words were spoken – not even a picture of any spiritual consequence came into my mind. My high expectations of the morning were unfulfilled and I was seriously doubting the authenticity of those spiritual writers from the desert. I went home.

The next morning I sat down to try and analyse what had happened and to see if this retreat business was worth pursuing. I began to see that besides the negatives, there were in fact some little encouragements. During that last half hour I had once or twice entered into a deep silence as if I was in God and He was somehow in me. It was similar to a winter's evening when Mary and I sit opposite each other in front of a fire. Except for the ticking of the clock the house is silent. For long periods we don't speak to each other – we don't need to because from somewhere deep within us both we are communicating.

I decided to try the retreat again. That was six years ago. Now, when I am not travelling, Thursday finds me either in the poustinia in The Grail garden or, in the extreme cold of winter, in a room in the main house.

As I went, week by week, a number of matters began to clarify themselves. The first concerned the culture I lived in and its subtle effect on my life. Most of us are caught up in a bustle of activity and noise. I see the commuters driving past our door on their way to catch either the 7.12 or the 7.46, which will speed them to the city. Twelve hours later the same men return home from what, for many, will have been an extremely demanding day. Supper, family and community commitments follow, then bed, and back again on the treadmill. I realised that I also measured my worth in terms of activity. I sought to do those things which were expected of me and this left little time for listening to God.

As I have said, it was the evangelicals who introduced me to the daily morning 'quiet time'. I was encouraged to praise and thank God before asking for things. I was also taught that it was helpful to have a list of people and situations which could then be systematically prayed over. Having worked through this introduction there followed the Scripture Union daily reading notes. These suggested a passage of scripture, which I was to read, and gave a short devotional commentary. I had to fix the truth in my mind and, hopefully, this would in turn affect my behaviour. This system was continued to help countless thousands and its greatest strength is in its ability to instil discipline into the Christian life, without which there can be little spiritual growth. Yet the weakness is its emphasis on what we do – on our activity. I began to realise more than ever that it is God who wants to take the initiative with us. He, in Carlo Caretto's terms, is the 'God who comes'. The praise and thanksgiving should then be our response to His presence. David, the Psalmist, had come to this understanding when, on a number of occasions, he sang about waiting patiently for the Lord.

At The Grail I sit quietly and seek the Lord, and I find that He comes to me in non-verbal ways. It is as if His Spirit touches my spirit and at times I sing or dance for joy. After such moments the Scriptures really come alive and many a new thought begins to come to delight my soul.

I came to realise that in moments of anxiety there had to be a giving to Christ and an actual receiving from Him. For me, a crucial verse is found in Philippians 4:6 where Paul repeats the admonition of Jesus concerning anxiety. He writes: 'Do not be anxious about anything, but in everything, by prayer and petition, with thanksgiving, present your requests to God. And the peace of God, which transcends all understanding, will guard your hearts and your minds in Christ Jesus.'

Anxiety had always been something which had bugged me. I have tried in practical ways to put Paul's command into effect. Often in the morning I would sit down with a blank piece of paper and jot down all the situations causing me anxiety. Once listed, I would talk to the Lord about each one before crossing it off the list. This has been my discipline for many years, but in the poustinia I discovered the missing ingredient. After sharing with the Lord, I found I needed just to wait and receive His peace. Previously I used to rush on to my next commitment, so often taking the feelings of anxiety with me. To describe the receiving of peace is impossible, but I began to learn that it was certainly a possibility.

The quietness showed me how conditioned I am not only to activity, but also to noise. Our family is part of a noise orientated culture. At 6.30 a.m. the radio goes on in Tim's room, followed half an hour later by Jonathan's and Noonie's. By 7 a.m. we have Radio 1 in triple sound! If the world of our teenagers is filled by pop music, then the adult world is filled by news national and news international, news background, news specialists and in-depth studies of the news, commencing at 6.00 a.m. and going on until lights out.

I found that I was so conditioned to noise that initially silence became a threat. Silence allowed the unpalatable truths of life to raise their ugly heads. Unhelpful attitudes held against other people could no longer be ignored. Neither could situations in my life which I had repressed and tried to forget. I discovered in the silence that many experiences of the past were re-lived. Repentance was made and inner healing received.

Setting aside a weekly day of solitude also created great expectancy in other areas of prayer. Mary and I have now been married twenty years and in the early days we found praying together difficult. It was not until we were filled by

the Holy Spirit that this changed. At that time we reviewed
our spiritual life and decided, when possible, to arise at 6.00
a.m., have an hour's prayer individually, then come together
for a corporate time. This discipline has been the mainstay of
our Christian life.

When we pray together we seek to bring to the Lord our
thanksgiving and all that the day may hold. Mary is a clinical
teacher at a hospital for the terminally ill, and often we
will intercede for individuals or groups for which she has
responsibility. Always we pray for our family and the known
needs of each one. Our family life never seems to have been
straightforward and, in the midst of the many turmoils, we
are learning to seek the Lord.

We have learned together that the Lord always answers
prayers, yet in our experience it is very much according to the
promise of Jesus in His teaching on prayer in Luke 11. He
said: 'Ask and it will be given to you; seek and you will find;
knock and the door will be opened to you.' Here we have the
promise of an answer – an answer which comes through
seeking – and finally one which comes through patiently
waiting.

On one occasion, our second son, Timothy, who was at the
end of his fifth year, having taken his 'O' levels, asked us to
pray for a challenging summer job. Amongst other needs on
that particular morning, we asked the Lord's help for this.
We had scarcely finished our prayer when the telephone rang
– the time was 7.10 a.m. and we wondered who could be
calling so early. It turned out to be our friend Chris Bean who
runs a Fishermen's Co-operative based on the Helford River.
He asked whether Timothy could spend the summer with
him preparing fish for export.

Illness in the family is always worrying and from a very
early age Timothy had suffered from chronic asthma. When
an attack came on him Mary and I would pray, and over a
period of nearly seven years we spent hours interceding to the
Lord for him. Often in the middle of a particularly bad attack
we knew an immediate breaking of it as we prayed, but the
cause was never dealt with. In the autumn of 1976 the attacks

reached an all time high, which meant many days off school.
At 3 a.m. one morning he appeared in our bedroom gasping
for breath. We called our doctor who came immediately with
an injection to break the sequence. We continued to pray and
the eventual breakthrough came when, on the evening of the
Harvest Festival, Timothy asked the church to pray for him.
He told us he experienced a heat which flowed into his lungs
and, whatever the cause was, that night the Lord dealt with it
once and for all.

I shall never forget the time I first fasted. I was to be
priested in Truro Cathedral. With a number of others I spent
the days at the Community of the Epiphany, a little order of
Anglican nuns which the then Bishop described as the
spiritual powerhouse of his diocese. I always hoped that this
was an episcopal exaggeration as only about two of the sisters
were not bedridden or in the retirement home! On arrival I
announced to Sister Rosemary that I would be fasting.

Within an hour of missing the first meal the dear Sister was
at my door enquiring after my state of health. This happened
at regular intervals during the first day. After missing breakfast the next morning, the Archdeacon and Bishop were both
informed. By lunchtime I was under so much pressure that I
thought, in order to avoid any more difficulties, I would call
the fast off. My announcement sent a sigh of relief through
the whole community and a special supper was cooked for me
which, in quantity, made up for all that I had missed!

It was consequently with a certain amount of
apprehension that on these Thursdays I felt it right to have
another try. It was my intention initially to miss Wednesday
supper and fast until Thursday supper. Except for Mary, no
one else was involved, so the practical problem was solved.

As the weeks went by I fasted as a discipline, and then I
had a concern which led me into my first week's fast. I had
read articles on the coming of cable TV and the use of
satellites which would give the average home a large choice of
local and foreign channels. My concern was how Christians
could capitalise on this situation and present Christ in a
contemporary way. I decided to fast and pray to this end.

Because this was my first major fast I decided each evening to write down the events of the day. I didn't have any preconceived ideas of how the time should be spent or what God would say. However, I was slightly taken aback by what happened during the first two days. Normally I don't remember dreams, but during this time I had two very vivid ones.

In the first dream I was with Mary. We were both younger and had just started to develop a relationship. As the relationship grew she was prepared for a friendship but would not commit herself to anything permanent. I awoke, beside myself with grief, and wondered why she had rejected me. During the day the Lord used this dream to unearth areas of rejection. As I visualised these I felt God taking away the pain they had caused.

When I was a student I used to trap opossum for their skins. With friends I would set a line of twenty or thirty traps along the tracks which the opossum used. Early in the morning we would empty the traps and skin those which had been caught the previous day. To kill these animals I had a piece of steel pipe and would hit them behind the ears. After becoming a Christian this began to trouble me and I would not allow myself to think about what I had done. On the second night I dreamed vividly about these episodes and awoke with feelings of guilt and fear. Again it was as if the Holy Spirit had used the nightmare to release me from the destructive thoughts associated with the killings.

Physically these first two days were difficult. A continuous ache dulled my head and my body felt weak and cold. At this stage I was becoming preoccupied with food and I wanted to end the fast. However, I decided to continue it and spent the week meditating on the prophecy of Joel. I found myself being moved to repentance as I realised how much I was part of the very things God was condemning through the prophet.

Wednesday was a turning point. Within my heart there was a desire to seek the Lord, and I spent much of my time sitting quietly in His presence. I found that He put thoughts in my mind which I was able to respond to with joy and thanksgiving. During the day I started to intercede for the opportunity for Christians to respond creatively to television opportunities of the future.

By the weekend I felt as if a barrier had been broken and I was aware of another reality. I often jog in the mornings across the local common. On the hard cold winter mornings I run towards a copse where bare frosted branches are silhouetted against the first light of day. Suddenly the sun's rays strike the branches and within minutes I am in a world of wonder. As the light enhances awareness of the natural world, so a long fast enhances awareness of the spiritual world.

Before I started preaching I used to be fascinated by the way well-known preachers received their message from God. In his diaries George Whitefield wrote of the times he spent prostrate on the floor seeking to hear a word from God. Likewise Billy Graham wrote of how he walked alone in the mountains of North Carolina seeking God's message for a particular occasion.

When I left theological college I had only preached two sermons from a church pulpit. As final year students we were divided into sermon classes under a tutor. Each week one would preach while the others listened. Then we would return to college and discuss what we had heard. When my turn came I had no idea how to begin. Our college was near Goldhill Baptist Church where David Pawson was pastor. I went to hear him. David was expounding the book of Romans and had come to the passage in which Paul wrote that he was not ashamed of the gospel because it was the power of God for salvation to all who believed.

After the service I ordered the tape and laboriously copied out his hour-long sermon. I decided to limit myself to verse 16 of Romans 1, which had taken him twenty-five minutes to expound. During the next week I went over the sermon numerous times until I had learnt it off by heart. Sunday came and we went to a village church where I delivered my soul to twelve elderly ladies, the verger, the sermon class and Michael Green my tutor.

Back at Michael's home we sat drinking coffee whilst Michael asked for comments on my sermon. He was intrigued by its composition. He had not failed to note that I had four major headings, each beginning with the letter 'B'. He thought the illustrations were excellent, and the sermon most encouraging. Fellow students added their comments and then Michael looked at me and asked whether I had prepared the sermon myself.

For my next sermon I sat down for what seemed hours with a Bible and a blank piece of paper, waiting for God to speak. Nothing seemed to come; so I resorted to a Billy Graham sermon on being 'born again'. I learned it by heart and preached it in the same idiom as Billy. My tutor was seated in the front and, whenever I caught his eye, he had his index finger to his lips. He was trying to tell me to lower my voice. When I finished I asked the congregation to bow their heads. After a prayer, I invited those so moved to come forward during the final hymn and receive Christ.

On the Monday morning I was summoned to the Principal's study. As I arrived the vicar of the parish I had visited had just left. He had apparently been furious. He didn't believe in being 'born again' and found my style insensitive and my fundamentalism abhorrent. As far as he was concerned, his congregation would never again be dummies for students such as me to preach at.

When I moved to Cornwall I was expected to preach every Sunday. While there I discovered the sermons of the German theologian and preacher, Helmut Thielicke. Each week I would study one of his sermons and commit it to memory. If I wasn't preaching other people's material I would take a passage of Scripture and, using as many commentaries as I could find, I would put a sermon together. However, I kept coming back to the diaries of men that God had used in the past. A common feature seemed to be that they had heard God and their preaching came out of a word from Him.

In the poustinia I gradually became aware that God was speaking to me. I realised He had also spoken in the past but I had just not heard Him. I had always thought that hearing

God meant hearing an audible voice. Then I noticed that on Mt Carmel God spoke to Elijah through a cloud the size of a man's fist. Whilst he watched it, it increased in size until it filled the whole sky. I discovered that, in the quietness, the still small voice of God is at times like the tiny cloud. It comes as a seed thought, or from a meditation upon the Scripture. As we dwell on this the Holy Spirit increases its meaning. He also puts the burden of that message upon our hearts so that at times we know no peace until we have preached it.

Whilst ministering in the Indian state of Kerala I found myself speaking at a conference with Bishop Timotheous from the Mar Thoma Church. His message was simple, but delivered with great power and gentleness. I had seldom heard such a relevant message to the troubled heart of man. During our time together I quizzed him about this. He told me that, before he preached, it was his habit to wait upon God for the theme. He would then spend two or three hours meditating upon the relevant Scriptures. When he spoke he never used notes; he trusted the Holy Spirit to remind him of the message which he had assimilated during the time he had spent sitting quietly with God.

I find that my days spent in the poustinia have not become easier with the passing of time. It is always a struggle to be still, and many thoughts battle to control the mind. However, it has become a haven where I set time aside to try and hear God's word for the places to which I believe He is sending me.

Chapter 9

IN THE CITY

In Christian circles the idea of God being 'in action' in dark primitive Africa, or amongst the poor and illiterate of India, is a concept readily accepted. Books of missionary work have long been passed around our congregations and Christians have been greatly stirred by the accounts of physical healing and deliverance from demons. However, the problem has always been to connect these stories with what actually happens in the life of the average parish church. During our visits to churches in this country we are seeing that God can do the same here as He has always seemed to be doing there.

Chris Wood invited us to Holy Trinity, Parr Mount, St Helens. In 1969 most of the area had been demolished to make way for the A58 which now runs past the vicarage front door. Gone were the rows and rows of terraced council houses, and many of their inhabitants had moved to Haydock, Eccles and Sutton. The main view from the vicarage lounge is that of a large gasometer towering above the new council housing, emphasising the fact that the Victorian church and school are monuments to an age which has long since passed away. The majority of people had been employed in the nearby Pilkington glass factory but, with the recession, one in seven have found themselves without a job and with little prospect of getting another.

At various times the Liverpool diocese had tried to close the church and amalgamate the parish with a neighbouring one. This move had always been strongly opposed by a nucleus in the church and eventually a compromise was

reached with the appointment of a priest-in-charge. Spiritually it had always been a difficult parish; the Rev Eric
Hague (Chris Wood's predecessor) accepted it as his last
challenge before retiring. This Spirit-filled man had spent
much of his ministry abroad with the China Inland Mission.

For four years Eric sought to bring the church into renewal, but was thwarted at every turn. The congregation had
a 'low church' tradition which they rigorously defended.
According to the minutes of his last annual meeting in 1979
Eric is on record as saying that in over forty years of his
ordained ministry, Holy Trinity church had been the hardest
place he had ever had to work.

When Chris Wood arrived to be priest-in-charge of the
parish, he asked one of the stalwarts why it was that none of
his predecessors had lasted more than four years. The reply
was simply: 'We see them off!' This curt response gave Chris
a grim insight into the challenge which lay ahead. Nevertheless he took up the challenge, full of an enthusiasm which was
soon to wane. The Church Council, two thirds of whom lived
outside the parish, rigidly opposed any suggestion of change.
In desperation he invited a group of eight from the congregation to go on a conference for lay leaders to York, where
Chris himself had recently experienced renewal. He hoped
that this group would become a nucleus for change. However, they were unable to relate what they experienced at York
to their own situation and had nothing to suggest when they
returned.

After two years Chris felt that he had tried everything
without success and realised that, unless God did something
dynamic, there was little use in remaining there. For two
months he went through a period of dark spiritual depression. In this frame of mind he went to the Anglican Renewal
Ministries conference in Swanwick, hoping to find some
glimmer of hope. On the first evening he sat next to Iain
Roberts. As they sat together Iain described the Faith Sharing Ministry and told Chris of the ways in which we had
begun to experience God in action. Within six months we
were at Holy Trinity.

Our conference was held on an extremely cold late November Saturday in the hall of a disused church school. Two gas fires did their best, but our guitarists still needed their gloves, with the fingers cut out, to keep warm enough to play.

During the morning session I noticed Andrew who looked as if he was becoming uncomfortably hot which, considering the circumstances, seemed strange! Perspiration beads glistened on his brow and he periodically unbuttoned yet another piece of clothing. Just before lunch I stopped and encouraged those present to welcome the Holy Spirit afresh into their lives. As I looked at Andrew I sensed the Lord saying that He was healing him of an ulcer. I walked to where he was sitting and asked him what was happening. He replied that his stomach felt as if it was full of burning coals. From our conversation it transpired that he had suffered from an ulcer for many years and kept this in check by doses of medicine and tablets.

On the Saturday evening our team divided up and led meetings based on people's homes. At the team meeting the following morning we shared together what God had done in our particular meetings. Dennis and Miriam reported that they had had a man at theirs who got so hot as the evening progressed that he ended up with his shirt wet through with perspiration. This was Andrew again. I was looking forward to finding out what had happened to him during the night.

On the Sunday morning he came to worship looking much more relaxed and happy. He told me that his stomach still felt full of heat and every time he began to pray or praise the Lord the heat would flow through the whole of his body. By the Sunday evening all pain and discomfort had gone and he was feeling very well indeed. Two weeks later I telephoned Chris to find out what had happened to him. Apparently Andrew had stopped all medication and was so thankful to be well after so many years of pain.

After I had spoken with Andrew that Sunday morning I asked all those who would like prayer to indicate by a show of hands. Many did. John misunderstood and stood up in the midst of the meeting. He was an older man who told me that he thought I had said, 'If you would like prayer for healing, stand up'. Owing to a nasal condition he had not been able to smell for twenty years and, as he stood, he felt heat resting in the nasal area of his face. This surprised him and, while he wondered what could be happening, he found that his sense of smell had returned. Even the smell of a dirty hall was a joy after so many years.

When the Holy Spirit came upon Joyce she fell to the floor resting in His presence. For those who have never witnessed such things before this can be rather alarming. She lay at the side of the hall for nearly two hours. During that time I noticed that periodically her face was distorted and she became quite agitated. On other occasions her lips moved quickly as if speaking, yet no words were heard. This experience had a profound effect on her.

Joyce's husband, Ron, had been unemployed for nine years and as a result her life had been full of tensions. She and Ron had decided to have a meeting in their home that evening and she left the hall to invite the whole of her family and many friends to come. Arthur and Shirley from our team led the evening and at the end all those present knelt and asked Jesus to be real to them in their lives.

Chris felt that this weekend was a turning point in the life of the church. Many people had experienced the power of God in their lives, whilst many others had either seen God in action or heard the testimonies of those whose lives had been touched by His Spirit. Some also saw the possibilities of sharing their faith in their homes as a number of their friends had come to know Christ during the Saturday evening.

For our team this visit was also a landmark. We had been to many inner-city churches and urban areas, and we now began to feel that an extension of our visits might be for members of the team to move into such areas and help local believers to build the church.

Returning to Chorleywood I began to pray about our future involvement with Holy Trinity, as Chris had invited us to return later for another two weeks. Whenever I prayed a thought kept coming to my mind. Initially I discarded it as it

involved Bob and Mary Gardner-Hopkins from our neighbouring parish, Christ Church in Chorleywood. Bob had just
been ordained in the ministry as a non-stipendiary minister.
He is a gifted Bible teacher and Mary has a counselling
ministry. Besides that they are excellent communicators and
very much involved in our weeks of outreach. I had come to
rely on them in our travelling ministry as good standbys. I
thought that maybe the Lord wanted them to move to Parr
Mount on a permanent basis.

I shared this idea with Chris and he was overjoyed by the
prospect. He asked them to join him in the parish. Within
months Bob had resigned his job as an accountant and
together they had moved from their lovely home in Chorleywood into a little terraced house without a view. All this had
the generous support of David Saville, the vicar of Christ
Church.

I was apprehensive about our return visit. I wondered how
a middle-class suburban team would relate for two weeks in a
working-class parish. We, who could afford to take time off
work, would be staying with families who could well be living
on the dole. Besides this, I felt unsure about what aspect of
the gospel we should be seeking to communicate.

On my regular Thursday in the poustinia I shared all my
concern in prayer and waited upon the Lord. During this
time I thought of the city of Corinth and how Paul had taken
the gospel to the people there. He said that at his meetings he
had decided to talk about nothing else except the death of
Jesus on the cross. This was it: our theme would be 'The
Cross'.

When we returned we found that the ripples of new life had
spread into many areas of the parish. The staff had preached
a sermon series on 'Signs and Wonders' and many had been
touched by God in new ways. A group was meeting regularly
in the vicarage to pray. We found a sense of excitement and
expectancy when we arrived.

Our first service of worship was held in the daughter
church. I had asked that a full size cross be erected at all our
meetings and it completely overshadowed the room. Above

the horizontal bar was a small plaque on which was written
'Jesus, King of the Jews', and red paint depicted the places
where the nails had pierced both hands and feet.

After I had spoken, I invited people to come to the cross.
Both young and old gathered. Ted and his wife were the first.
Ted was in his late fifties and a non-churchgoer but he
wanted to believe in Jesus.

Craig had quite a different reaction. Accompanied by a lot
of noise he left the church in great anger. Chris followed him
out and discovered him striding up the road, looking for
someone to whom he could be violent. After placating him
somewhat, Chris coaxed him back into the church. As Craig
started to walk towards the cross, Prue, one of the team,
intercepted him and asked if he would like her to pray for him
that he might know Jesus. Craig nodded that he would and,
just as Prue was about to lay hands on him, he fell prostrate
on the floor, creating almost as much noise again as he had on
his way out of the church. Within the hour the peace of God
had so flooded his heart that, in his own words, he felt like a
new person.

The front rooms of the council houses in Parr Mount are
very small and twelve people are an incredible squash.
People have to sit on the floor, against the fireplace or even up
the stairs. We had a week of meetings in such rooms where we
and the local Christians were able to share our faith with
friends and neighbours. By Wednesday evening quite a
number had had an experience of Christ and I organised
discipleship meetings in the vicarage – the only place with a
large enough room – for the Thursday and Friday evenings.

Many of those converted had little or no Christian background. I talked this over with Tim, a young man from St
Andrew's, Chorleywood, who had also moved up to the area
to help in the church there. Tim had a gift for leading worship
and we decided that our starting point for the new Christians
would be teaching them to worship God.

By the time the meeting was under way the vicarage
lounge was crowded. I invited people to share what God had
done for them. Tim gave a short teaching on Christian

worship, stressing that the New Testament word most frequently used meant 'coming towards – to kiss'. He asked us to stand and we began to worship the Lord. After about ten minutes, a lady suddenly called out, 'I am seeing – I am seeing!' I moved quietly to the back of the room where Elsie was standing, dressed in black. She had come to Christ the previous evening in one of the meetings. Her husband had deserted her and she had been left to bring up two sons. Many years before she had become blind in her left eye but now she told me that as she began to worship, light had flooded into her blind eye. She also found herself weeping – something she had not done for years. Elsie's healing was gradual. At the public meeting the following week she started to see shapes and by the second week she received greater clarity still, but it was a whole year before her sight was completely restored.

Elsie was known locally as 'the lady in black' because of the clothes she wore. But within a few days of coming to Christ she had bought herself some new beautiful coloured replacements.

At that vicarage meeting the Holy Spirit fell powerfully upon all the young Christians and they continued to praise and worship God far into the night. After the worship the next evening we introduced the Bible and explained that our faith needed to be focused on Jesus and firmly planted in the promises which He has made in the word of God.

The following week we had meetings in Holy Trinity Church entitled 'God in Action'. Our format was simple. For the first forty minutes we worshipped the Lord. After this we had a time for people to tell of the ways in which they had come to experience Jesus. I followed this by preaching and then invited the Holy Spirit to minister to the people.

During the evening we invited people forward to the cross where our team prayed for them. On the first evening a young man, who was sitting at the back, started to walk towards the front of the church. As he approached the sanctuary where the cross was standing, he fell face downwards on the floor and started to weep. His whole body

moved in a series of contortions as he groaned in deeper and
deeper agony. Bob and Shirley went and knelt beside him.
Within a short while they too were weeping. It was as if they
were entering into his suffering.

For eighteen months this young man had lived on nothing
more than sugar. He had no work and spent most of his time
lying on his bed. The house from which he came was a centre
to which people in the area gathered during the day to watch
video nasties. On some occasions he had been so fearful that
he had to hide behind the sofa, only daring to follow the film
in short, sharp glances. His brother, who had been recently
released from prison, would at times torture him, leaving him
in pain and extremely frightened.

Eventually the convulsions subsided and the peace of God
came upon him. The next morning Bob and Mary arranged
to get him to their home for breakfast. They continued their
ministry to him for some time and, as a result, he continued
to grow and gain physical as well as spiritual strength.

Betty, a middle-aged lady, came for prayer with a trouble-
some arthritic condition which brought about swelling in
both her knees. As we prayed I had a 'word of knowledge' to
the effect that the condition was the result of something that
had happened to her son. It transpired that a number of years
previously he had been convicted of a criminal offence and
sentenced to four years' imprisonment. This young man was
her only child and the whole thing had devastated her.
Within weeks of his going to gaol she began to feel pain in her
knees. This became increasingly severe and left her crippled.

When we prayed we asked that Jesus would bind up her
broken heart. As the Holy Spirit began to minister, she
experienced feelings of heat, intensifying in her knees. The
following evening she described what had happened. Leaving the meeting she felt relieved, but still in some pain. In bed
that night she thanked the Lord for His healing power and
suddenly it was as if dozens of hot needles were moving in
and out of her knees. She lay peacefully as the prickling
sensations continued, eventually stopping in the early hours
of the morning. Stepping out of bed she discovered to her

delight that her knees had returned to normal and every vestige of pain had gone. Much to the amusement of the gathering that night, she lifted up her skirt so that we could all see what God had done to her knees.

During the meetings there were dozens of instances of people like Betty whose real problems were emotional. Others had stepped outside the boundaries which God has set for mankind and were suffering for it. One man told me that he was an addict. I thought he meant that he was dependent upon drugs or alcohol, but it was something equally destructive. Some years before he had gone to one of the local men's drinking sessions where pornographic films were shown. He found that he was unable to stop going and followed these sessions by reading pornographic magazines. His marriage was in pieces and his mind was in torment because he could only think about what he was seeing and reading. As he asked Jesus to set him free he felt 'a presence' leave his body.

Some months later we invited Chris to bring a team back to our church and minister at a special weekend we were hosting. During the Saturday afternoon Chris spoke and the team told of how they had come to know Jesus and the working of His Spirit. They concluded by leading a most inspiring time of worship. As they prayed for others it was obvious that the Holy Spirit was powerfully present and working through them. A number of their team also experienced God in new ways. At the final meeting on the Sunday one of the drivers was so drunk with the Spirit that he was unable to drive home. When they eventually left us in their vans, we could hear songs of praise from the edge of the Common.

Yet the next Sunday hardly any of them attended their own church. I have already described how I myself suffer from emotional reaction after a mission. In areas such as this where many have been emotionally battered by the events of life, people are often very unstable. One day they will readily talk about the new life Christ has brought them, but the next they are denying it and are violent to their partners. This type of behaviour puts heavy demands upon the pastoral leadership, as they have to visit regularly and encourage those who have fallen away.

When I meet the leadership of a church, I make it plain that they must be prepared to give away all they receive. This is a spiritual principle: 'Freely you have received, freely give' (Matt. 10:8). If we hold on to what God gives us, then the blessing will soon fade and become of little use. I suggest that a parish which receives our ministry must be open to the possibility of taking a team of their own to another church. Chris and the congregation readily responded to this challenge, and now regularly visit churches and groups in other inner city areas.

An extension of our team ministry came with an invitation from Cecil Kerr to tour a number of towns in Ireland. For ten years Cecil and Myrtle have led a community based in Rostrevor. At this Christian Renewal Centre, set in a place of great natural beauty, people of every religious and political background come together to meet God. This trip was to set a pattern for the future.

Chapter 10

TRAVELLING TOGETHER

I learnt a lot about the working of the Holy Spirit during my first experience of windsurfing in France in 1980. Our home group had planned a camping holiday, and on one occasion we were picnicking by a lake. We decided to hire a wind-surfer, and it was suggested that I should have first try. It seemed so easy! I balanced on the board, pulled up the sail, and a light breeze took me across the lake. Approaching the far side at increasing speed I realised it was becom-ing necessary to turn around. Time ran out and I crashed into the tree-lined bank. For the next hour I tried to extract myself, but to no avail. Eventually I paddled the board back to my friends who greeted me with resounding cheers.

This disastrous experience in France made me want to master the art of board sailing; so on returning home I went to local instruction classes. At the introductory lesson my instructor said, 'I shall teach you about the wind, but you must learn to know the wind.'

With the use of a blackboard and model he proceeded to teach me what the wind would do and how I was to adjust the board accordingly. For the next four weeks I spent more time in the water than on the board. However, I was slowly learning to know the wind and to discover its actions.

One summer Mary and I holidayed at Cornwall and I took the board on to the Helford River. The wind was force 4 and blowing off the land. Suddenly I realised what my instructor had meant. I was perfectly balanced and literally flying down the river with the spray cascading over my head which was poised a few feet above the water. I was learning how I should respond to the dictates of the wind.

This experience became a parable to me. Not long after the arrival of John Wimber and his team, I studied the Gospels to see what Jesus had taught about the Holy Spirit, and in the light of that tabulated the ways in which the early Christians had experienced Him. Through this I saw more clearly what had been happening at St Andrew's.

The Spirit, like the wind, blows where He wills and His ways of doing things are sometimes far removed from what we understand to be decent and orderly. During our first trip to Ireland I found myself particularly perplexed by the working of the Holy Spirit. Thankfully, I had a team of ten with me, and after each meeting we were able to discuss the various phenomena which people were apparently experiencing.

We started our tour of Ireland by ministering at a Church of Ireland National Renewal Conference based on University College, Dublin. David and Mary Pytches had flown to Dublin, but nine of us had travelled by car as we were going to minister in various towns after the Dublin meeting. We arrived on the evening of the first day of the conference, just as David had concluded his keynote address on 'The Kingdom of God'. The chapel was nearly full of clergy and their wives and other church leaders who had gathered from all over Ireland.

Standing with David I could see by the way people were reacting that the Holy Spirit was beginning to fall on many of the delegates. A number rested under His power. Words of knowledge were given and those to whom they related were invited forward for prayer. I noticed some people who were gently crying; others were shaking, and many were in deep communion with God. A lady who had arrived at the meeting with swollen arthritic knees testified to having been healed, as did a number of others. A majority stood perplexed.

The Primate of All Ireland, John Armstrong, sat in the

front row surrounded by fellow bishops and clergy. I sensed
that what was beginning to happen had not been his experience before. He looked around the chapel, then spoke to
those on his right and left. Suddenly he knelt and the men
with whom he had spoken laid hands on him and prayed.
Very soon after he too was praying with others. The healings
were a sign of the presence of Christ, as was this act of
humility.

Following the conference in Dublin, Willy Stewart had
organised a weekend for our team based on his church. Part
of the programme included a barbecue for young people.
After we had consumed the sausages, the gathering moved to
a school gymnasium: an unusual venue for us. Normally we
ministered within the context of a church building or hall. Of
the two hundred present probably half had no Christian
commitment. We led a time of worship, then John and
Debbie, a young married couple on our team, shared how
they had been anointed by the Holy Spirit and what they had
seen Him doing as they ministered to others. At the conclusion I gave a short talk. By this time there was a certain
amount of conversation and disruptive behaviour around the
fringes of the meeting.

I concluded my address by saying that what we had shared
about Jesus Christ was either true or not, and the only way
that could be known was by asking the Holy Spirit to make
Jesus real. Above the hubbub I prayed simply, 'Holy Spirit, I
invite you to come and work among us.' Suddenly two young
men fell to the floor under His power, one of whom suffered
from an ulcerated mouth and tongue. He lay there, his mouth
moving in an involuntary way. A strange silence had come
over the place. You could have heard a pin drop! Quietly I
explained that what they were seeing was God working by
His Spirit. A sense of great awe came over the meeting. As
they saw the 'signs and wonders' some believed, but many
did not, though they were interested enough to join us at a
meeting the following day.

Christ Church was the centre for the next day's conference. In response to a word of knowledge, a lady came for

prayer who suffered from sciatica. For many years she had been intermittently crippled by an intense pain in her hip and thigh. Four of us were praying for her and in Jesus' name we welcomed the Holy Spirit to come and heal. After a few minutes I asked what she felt, and she replied that it was as if her leg was being pulled into the ground. As this happened she kept losing her balance and had to be held. This action continued for a few minutes, then she experienced a deep, penetrating heat in her thigh and a feeling that it was being manipulated. While this was going on we did not touch her physically, except to stop her falling at the end of the healing when she was thrown some inches into the air.

The following evening she gave her testimony to a healing. It was then that my colleague, the Rev Iain Roberts, described how he had operated hundreds of times on the sciatic nerve. Before doing so he had always hospitalised the patient and put him on traction for four weeks. It would seem that at the start of this healing the Holy Spirit did His own traction before healing.

When seeking God, we can so easily be deceived by our own desires and ambitions. Having had a number of rather bad failures in that direction, I try to keep what I'm feeling about a certain situation to myself and just see what happens. While praying for our trip to Coleraine – our next stop – I saw in my mind a beach upon which a medium sized wave reached its zenith then, with controlled power, rolled across the sand. After a slight pause, this was followed by two others. I sensed the Lord was saying that His Spirit was going to come in three waves during the meeting that evening.

Jim and Flo Munro welcomed us to the rectory. We found them a wonderful couple, full of faith and expectancy. Through the ministry of Cecil Kerr and the team from Rostrevor, they had both come into a new experience of the Holy Spirit and, as a result, had called the church to a period of outreach. The evangelist Jim Smith had recently visited them with a team of students from Oakhill Theological College. A feature of that outreach had been its preparation.

Jim laid a great emphasis on the need for prayer and encouraged the congregation to form prayer triplets to intercede for their friends and neighbours. These small groups were undergirded by a series of larger, early morning, meetings. God had moved powerfully by His Spirit, and over seventy adults had committed their lives to Christ. We were privileged to follow this.

We arrived at the large wooden hall to find people already putting out extra seating. In addition to many of Jim's own congregation there were many Christians from other denominations in the city. We began by worshipping the Lord and I then shared ways in which our team had seen the Lord working in people's lives. After my talk I asked everyone to stand and invited the Holy Spirit to work among us. It was then that I remembered the picture of the three waves. Suddenly two young women, who had come to know Christ in the outreach, fell under the power of the Spirit. For some this was slightly alarming as these two were positioned in the front row and disturbed a number of chairs as they slid to the floor. At this point a young man in his twenties walked forward. The Holy Spirit was obviously upon him and I was just about to bless what God had started to do when he fell backwards, landing with a thud which echoed around the hall. Those of us standing near felt the vibrations across the timber of the floor. A number who had never seen anything like it before thought that he had died. In fact, I had never seen anything quite as dramatic either, but I knew it was the Holy Spirit at work, and said so. It was all rather dramatic. Looking around the hall I could see the Holy Spirit resting upon many people.

The second wave was one of anointing for ministry. The Holy Spirit manifested His presence with sensations of heat, or currents of power, in many people's hands. I asked those affected in this way to come forward. As we began to pray with them it seemed as if an even greater anointing came upon them. By now our team was having words of knowledge and people began to walk forward in response. We began to pair off those who were needing healing with those who had been anointed. Clearly, the Holy Spirit was doing many wonderful things.

I looked back to see how the young man was, who had fallen so violently to the floor. He was now standing talking to my colleague, Iain. An emotional problem had been troubling him, and he asked Iain if he would pray with him about it. Hardly had Iain started to pray than there was another resounding crash and again he fell backwards like a falling tree in a pine forest. The following morning I was to see him again, and I asked if there had been any bruising or physical damage resulting from his experience but he had forgotten the episode. What was foremost in his mind now was the sense of healing and inner freedom which the experience had brought him.

By eleven the hall had partially emptied, and it was then that the third wave came. A number who were sitting at the back of the hall were affected this time. Billy and Ann were amongst them. Ann had been converted at the Oakhill mission and, as the Holy Spirit came upon her, she spoke in tongues and prophesied. The prophecy was in the form of a mime. With great tenderness she put one arm around her husband and the other around the waist of a friend. She then took the hands of others around her and raised her arms in an attitude of worship. All the while her eyes were closed and it seemed to me that in loving God and her neighbour she was acting out the first two commandments.

In a special way this was to be Billy's evening. It transpired later that as the Holy Spirit had come upon his wife, he had received Christ into his heart after what had been for him a long struggle. Billy was a canoe champion and his sport had left him with a recurring pain in a damaged knee. Later that evening a group of young couples, including John and Debbie from our team, went to Billy and Ann's home for coffee. It was there that John and Debbie prayed for his knee. He said that while they prayed he felt as if a syringe had been inserted and this was withdrawing something from his knee. Debbie asked him if there was any one activity which he was unable to perform with his knee, and Billy replied that it was kneeling, so she told him to bend his knee. To the joy of all concerned, Billy started doing knee bends with great enthusiasm around the lounge!

John and Debbie had also prayed for a lady of about fifty who was deaf in one ear. It attracted my attention as they seemed to have spent almost forty minutes with her, which seemed exceptionally long in view of the fact that our policy on these missions is not to counsel people but to pray for them. It transpired that for the first twenty minutes nothing seemed to have happened, and then she began to feel considerable pain in her inner ear. This was accompanied by some heat which intensified, but then gradually her hearing was restored.

I have found on these trips away that the days seem to stretch through the nights, and this evening was no exception. We arrived back at the rectory with Jim and Flo, where we found a message from Hector and Pearl. Their daughter, Karen, had developed a series of kidney complaints, and also suffered from general ill health. This case proved to be a further illustration of the fact that the presenting problem is often not the real problem that God wants to deal with.

Karen was asleep in bed when we arrived, and I felt it important that first we should pray for her mother. Pearl had also suffered from kidney disease and the previous year surgeons had removed one of her kidneys. This operation was the culmination of a lifetime of ill health. In the Spirit, I perceived that Pearl's own mother also had suffered from ill health. As we shared this insight, Pearl confirmed it. Like a curse, ill health had been transmitted from mother to daughter and then on to the next generation. In our prayers, we put the cross of Jesus between Pearl and her mother and broke this curse of illness. Slowly she was filled with the healing power of Jesus and felt an intense heat seeping into every area of her body.

Hector was not a committed Christian, but was happy for me to pray with him. He consequently testified to having felt something leaving his body. This 'something' had started in his stomach, travelled through his chest, and went out through the top of his head. However one understands such a subjective experience, he was left with a feeling of deep peace and well-being.

Next we prayed for them together, and then prayed for the power of the cross to be between Pearl and her daughter Karen. Only after this did we venture into the bedroom where the little girl was asleep. We knelt and prayed the healing of Jesus over her. She awoke and was quite startled to discover a strange man in her room, but after a little explanation she received all that Jesus was doing for her.

On our journey to Lurgan we stopped at various vantage points to enjoy the beauty of the coast and the sight of the Scottish islands in the distance. We clambered around the Giant's Causeway. In my mind I kept having an impression of a sea swell gradually building up to form one large breaker which crashed over the beach. Again I sensed that this was how the Lord intended to work in the meeting that evening.

The meeting was interdenominational. Together we enjoyed an extended time of worship. The team then shared what they had seen God doing during the previous ten days, and I spoke. As I invited the Holy Spirit amongst us I felt a sense of great urgency. It was as if the wave broke and I somehow knew that if people didn't respond at once, they would miss what God intended for them at that moment.

Anointing for healing came powerfully upon a number of people in the gathering. Many children were affected and began to praise God in tongues. We encouraged the sick and suffering to come forward and stand beside those on whom the Holy Spirit rested so powerfully. Iain called an eleven-year-old boy to pray with him for a man who had damaged his leg and undergone surgery to little or no effect. Iain asked the boy to place his hands upon the man's knee and together they prayed. As heat is often a sign of the healing presence of the Spirit, Iain asked the man if he was feeling anything. He replied in the negative but said that he had already been healed. At the end of the evening Iain, in his capacity as a medic, examined his knee and found it completely whole.

God was obviously giving people the gift of faith, enabling

them to believe that He could work in miraculous ways. Debbie found herself with a small elderly lady who was obviously sitting in great discomfort. Her knee was swollen and very painful. Debbie spoke to the condition in the name of Jesus, and as she did this the lady was immediately healed.

Debbie's husband, John, found himself ministering to a lady in her early fifties who was full of arthritis. Every visible joint of her body was swollen and the pain was at times intense. As John called down the Holy Spirit upon her she felt heat in her shoulders. She then fell down under the Spirit and during that time he prayed for all the affected joints. Within a short while she was up on her feet, claiming that all the pain and swelling had gone.

Some people were perplexed and a number left at the first opportunity. However, quite a few who had observed what had happened stayed, requesting prayer, but by that time there was nothing like the previous anointing and reality of God. Everything seemed hard work, with little visible manifestation of the Spirit's presence. The wave had rolled on.

Finally we went to Lisburn Cathedral where Bishop Ban It Chou, formerly of Singapore, joined our team for the Saturday conference. By this time the team had grown to twenty as members of the community at Rostrevor were also joining us at our various venues. I encouraged our team to take turns in describing some of the signs and wonders which they had seen in the meetings. After the testimonies I tried to answer some of the questions raised by what was said, and finished my talk by asking for 'words of knowledge' – insights from God about any people present. A word was given relating to a lady with a pain in the top of her back and right shoulder. She walked forward and, as John and Debbie prayed with her, the healing came immediately. She told them that she had experienced a physical release and instantaneous relaxation of her back. We then prayed with a number of people whom the Lord was anointing to heal, and they in turn started to minister alongside our team as people came forward.

At this meeting God began a work which was to reach its

full circle back in Chorleywood. Alex and Maureen come from a parish near Lisburn where Alex is a vicar. Because of the pressure of work, he was unable to go to the Dublin conference, but was delighted that Maureen could make the trip. Maureen had suffered all her life from a congenital heart condition which meant, amongst other restrictions, that she was unable to sleep while lying on her left side. At the Dublin conference she had been prayed with and found that her heart had settled down into a natural rhythm and, for the first time, that night she had been able to sleep on her left side.

During the day it occurred to Alex that maybe the Lord would heal him too. He suffered from a rare blood disease and had to go to hospital every three weeks to have blood tests. We met him at Lisburn and he began to feel hope rising within his heart. A few months later Alex and Maureen were holidaying in Hertfordshire and on the first Sunday they came to St Andrew's. I joined them after the service, and so did George who is in charge of welcoming newcomers. Alex asked us if we would pray for his condition. Again we called upon the Holy Spirit, and waited. I had a strange 'word of knowledge' relating to car accidents.

It transpired that Alex had once been a rally driver and had been involved in a number of frightening scrapes with cars. There was one accident which was particularly traumatic. We started to pray about this accident and asked Jesus to release the shock which still seemed to be trapped within him. Bob Maynard then prayed about the blood condition and Alex began to sense the power of God within his body.

On the third Sunday of their holiday they came to the marquee which was erected on the Common at the end of July for our United Churches Children's Holiday Week. In the evening we used it for combined services. David Pytches was leading the meeting, and invited Alex and Maureen to give their testimony. Alex had been for a medical check up locally and his blood condition was reported to be normalising remarkably.

In this chapter I have deliberately chosen to write about the more sensational aspects of what happened in Ireland. I found much to perplex me. However, we were able to talk over these events as a team after each meeting, and to learn together how the Holy Spirit operates. It was also here that new insights into team ministry started to emerge.

Firstly it seemed important to have a team of people who were not only open to God but also able to relate well together. Irrespective of what we say or do, what we are is our main witness to the gospel of Christ. If we are not loving each other it will quickly become apparent. In practice this involves immediately sorting out any misunderstandings which might arise. Often during a prayer time I will ask the team to stand in a circle, holding hands. Whilst we wait upon God I invite the Holy Spirit to minister to us. Periodically He brings to mind wrong attitudes. These we confess and put right.

Besides the ongoing need to keep loving relationships with each other, we find that the closeness of our fellowship can raise unresolved areas in our own lives. When the Holy Spirit is invoked, such healing needs can be revealed, and one of us might break down in tears. The team then prays. However, it is important that members of the team are not in the initial stages of being emotionally healed. If this were the case the team would be so taken up with a team member's needs that time and energy would be taken away from the major task of ministering to others.

On other occasions we may be praying for others during a meeting, and the workings of the Holy Spirit in the person with whom we are praying may trigger off a healing need in our own lives. When this happens I take the person concerned away from the immediate situation and arrange for others to pray with them when the meeting has finished.

An hour before every team engagement we meet to wait upon God. As far as we know how, we open our lives to Him asking for the anointing power of His Spirit. Next we pray for team members who will be making a special contribution. As the meeting proceeds we continue to support each other, often praying quietly in tongues.

It is my policy to give each team member every opportunity to develop their gifts. I also encourage full participation in the planning of a particular ministry. However, I expect each one to be under my leadership. This is important because, on some occasions, a meeting will develop differently from the way we had planned. As a result, new decisions need to be taken and those who have prepared material may not be able to give it.

Members must also be able to discipline the contribution I ask them to make. If I ask three people to talk, for eight minutes each, on an aspect of the Lord's work in their lives, it must be for the time stated. In some situations I have felt that the second person should share more; so at the end of their time I continue their contribution in the form of an interview. It could well be that we will not have the third testimony. This calls for humility.

I never find it particularly easy myself when friends suggest that I could improve the way I present a subject or lead a meeting. However, it is crucial that we should be able to give, receive, and implement justifiable criticism. If this does not happen in a team situation it can build up and create tension. I am a 'spontaneous' person, and I know my spontaneity can cause problems within a team. On one such occasion I sensed Peter was having difficulty with me. This simmered for a few days before I asked him what the problem was. He told me that he was delighted to do whatever I asked of him as long as I gave sufficient notice. He found being called upon to give a spontaneous contribution embarrassing and difficult.

This illustrates the need for a team leader to be sensitive to what each member of his team is able to contribute at any particular time. Another great mistake is to give a person more responsibility than he can cope with.

Our tour of Ireland lasted two weeks, but subsequently we have been away for six. This raises questions in many places where we minister. People often ask me how I can leave my family for such long periods. I always reply 'With great difficulty'! When an invitation is given to take a team on a long tour, I firstly ask Mary to pray about it. If she is happy, then I take the next step of submitting the invitation to David Pytches and our Standing Committee.

Mary and I have been happily married for twenty-one years. At the start of my travelling ministry I had hoped that she would be involved fully with me. However, the Lord led us in different ways. She felt that because God had called me, her first priority was to provide a secure base for me and our children. As our children grew and became independent, God opened another door for her.

Mary had qualified as a nurse and six years ago applied to go for a six-week course on the care of dying patients. This was based on Michael Sobell House attached to Mount Vernon Hospital in Northwood, Middlesex. At the completion of the course she was invited on to the staff, and now plans and leads the course she once was on. However, when her commitments permit, she now travels with me. We have a joke that she is usually available for the more exotic trips!

For such trips I find a team of ten to be the best size. The nucleus will be full-time members of the staff of the church. A number will be those who have retired early, and others will take holidays or negotiate special leave with their employers. Such teams, travelling from churches where God is pouring out His Spirit, are a key factor in taking the gospel to the world. The teams do not just take with them a gospel of words. They communicate a life-style which is being worked out in their home churches and also in the stress and difficulty of travelling. Above all, they minister a power which will be left in the places they visit. It is as if they take a burning coal from their home fireplace and place it anywhere in the world.

A number of foreign church leaders are seeing the advantages of such a team. Recently the Bishop of Karachi in Pakistan told our congregation that it was his opinion that such a team travelling through his diocese would be a better investment than traditional missionaries. The short stay team could minister through interpreters, and be involved with leaders and key churches in the diocese. Besides ministering the power of the Holy Spirit, the team could also train the congregations to minister in the same way.

It was some years before I was able to lead a team on an international tour. This was to New Zealand for six weeks. However, I began to realise the potential when I started to travel in India with an 'ad hoc' team drawn from different churches.

Chapter 11

INDIAN JOURNEY

I visited India for the first time in 1975. I was with Michael Harper and together we had the privilege of introducing the Church of South India to the charismatic renewal.

That trip proved to be extremely difficult. We spoke at clergy conferences in Hyderabad, Dijiwadi, Madras and Bangalore. The opposition came from the clergy who thought that the charismatic movement in the historic churches was the same as pentecostalism which they saw as divisive in their churches. Pentecostals taught doctrines which were contrary to the teaching of the Church of South India, maintaining that the only real baptism was for adults through total immersion. Pentecostals also insisted that no one could have been filled with the Holy Spirit if he did not speak in tongues. Some went as far as to say that unless you spoke in tongues you were not even a Christian.

Michael sought daily to combat this hostility with biblical teaching on the person and work of the Holy Spirit. A number of the clergy came into blessing, but the majority remained sceptical. However, two of the leading bishops accepted what God was doing. The first was Samuel, the Bishop of the Krishna diocese and Moderator of the Church of South India. Shortly after our visit his wife was tragically killed when a petrol bomb was thrown into his car. Bishop Samuel had been seeking to combat corruption which had come to light in his diocese and the culprit tried to kill him. The second was Sundar Clark, Bishop of Madras, with his wife Clara. What God had started to do in him was to have repercussions in many churches across India.

Although there was much opposition, we ended the visit on a 'high' note. Travelling overnight from Madras, we went by train down to the city of Madurai with its famous Hindu temple. Here we spent two days at the theological college. In the morning Michael lectured to the staff and students on what God was doing through the charismatic renewal. There was much interest and the afternoon was spent answering questions from thoughtful students. After the chapel service in the evening some 167 men with their wives waited behind for prayer, and many were powerfully filled with the Holy Spirit and received spiritual gifts.

In 1982 Michael and I were invited to speak at the first national renewal conference, which was held in Madras. It was there that we saw the harvest of our early years in India. The title for the theme they had chosen was 'Church Aflame'. Three hundred and fifty clergy and forty bishops had travelled from all parts of India to be present. The conference lasted four days with church leaders meeting during the day. There were public meetings each evening. On the first evening at least 12,000 packed into a school sports field to hear Mother Teresa of Calcutta give the opening address.

As she arrived I was sitting with others on the platform and so had a view out over the crowd. Dressed in her characteristic white and blue sari she looked diminutive, and her tiny frame stooped slightly as she walked to the microphone. Even before she spoke I found that I was in tears. So were nearly all the others on the platform and many many people in the crowd in front.

Bishop Sundar Clark introduced the founder of the Missionaries of Charity as the 'Mother of India'. The joy in her heart radiated from her eyes along deep lines in her face which broke into frequent smiles and laughter. However, from around her mouth there were other lines – which I observed from my position on the platform – deep creases of compassion which showed as she spoke of the poor, the

unloved and uncared for, lines which bore silent witness to
the tears and pain she had experienced on their behalf.

At the press conference late that afternoon she was fiercely
grilled by reporters who were trying to discover some ulterior
motive for her work amongst the poor. She spoke of the need
to identify with the poor if a real work was going to be done
amongst them. The temperature was in the hundreds and all
present were wet with perspiration. Upon the desk behind
which Mother Teresa was sitting was a bottle of water with a
glass. One of the reporters asked her if she would like to have
a break for a few moments and take a drink. I was profoundly
moved by her reply. She said that she never took food or
water before 5.00 p.m. as that was the only time in the
afternoon it was available to the poor amongst whom she
worked in Calcutta.

As she spoke on the theme of the conference she said that
spiritual renewal was to do with the heart. It involved falling
in love with Jesus and living for Him. To illustrate the point
of living for Jesus she told a moving story about a six-year-old
orphan boy. The Sister had rescued him from the streets of
Calcutta where he was dying of fever and nursed him back to
health. On the day that he was to leave for another home they
gave him a small packet of sugar – a highly prized commodity
amongst the poor. A quarter of a kilo of sugar equals a day's
wages. As the little boy walked through the gates he saw the
Sisters carrying in another child, obviously in great need. He
walked straight over to them and handed the sugar to the
Sisters, saying that he wanted the sick child to have it.
Mother Teresa asked him why he had done it. 'I think that is
what Jesus would have done,' he replied.

To illustrate how much God loves each one of us she
mentioned another case. In their home for the terminally ill
at Calcutta there was a beggar rescued from the gutter by the
Sisters. When they washed him they discovered flies' eggs in
the sores of his body and maggots feeding off his flesh. After
cleaning him thoroughly they bathed his wounds with anti-
septic. All this happened a few days before he died. A visiting
western journalist asked the Sister why they spent so much of

their time on someone who was so obviously about to die. It was suggested that it would have been better to leave the beggar in the street. Mother Teresa responded with the message of the cross and the love of God. She said that God has no favourites. He loves the dying, even a maggot-infested outcast, as much as she knew herself to be loved. She quoted the man's dying words: 'I have spent all my life as an animal on the streets, but today I am dying like an angel.'

Michael Harper and I returned to India in 1983 for the national renewal conference at Nagpur, and in February 1984 I went with Michael and Jeanne Harper, 'Chuck' Irish (vicar of St Luke's, Ohio) and his lay colleague, Bruce Folks, on a tour of Sri Lanka and southern India. The invitation to Sri Lanka had come from Bishop Swithian Fernando. The plan was to spend a week based on the parish of St Paul's, Miligiriya, a suburb of Colombo, and then lead a final weekend at the Cathedral of Christ, The Living Saviour.

We were hosted at various places and I stayed at St Margaret's Convent. It was here that I became conscious of the troubled atmosphere of the island. The Sisters had given a large section of their accommodation to Tamil families who had lost their homes and livelihood in the community violence. Many were very afraid and hardly ever left the compound to venture into the streets of the city.

The vicar of St Paul's, Miligiriya, the Rev Bala Arulpragasm, had experienced a physical healing in answer to prayer. Both he and his wife wanted to lead his church on in things of the Spirit. In the morning meeting Michael and Chuck had teaching sessions with clergy and Christian workers whom the Bishop had invited, and I spoke in the evening at the public meetings. It was here that we started to witness the Lord working through signs and wonders.

One man gave testimony to having been healed of a heart condition. He told of the difficulty he had had walking to the meeting the previous evening. He got out of breath very quickly and had to sit down frequently to recover. But when he walked home after the meeting he found the breathlessness had left him and he could feel a burning heat in his heart.

He said that he had run all the way from his home to the church this evening and finished his testimony anouncing loudly: 'I am a thousand times a thousand better!'

A Hindu girl told how she had come to know Christ. On the first evening she had been taken to the meeting by Sister Chandrani from the Convent. Before telling what happened on that night, she recounted her growing experience of God. She had left her home in one of the villages and found lodging in Colombo where she had to spend her last year as a trainee accountant. There were many people staying in the house in which she lodged, and no place where she could be alone to study. In fact, the people who ran the boarding house would only allow the lights on for an hour after sunset.

While walking out in the evening, she had seen a light on regularly in a room attached to the church. She wondered if she might be allowed to study there so she went to enquire. She had never been to a church before, but she found a pastor working behind a desk in a room which turned out to be his vestry. She asked him if it would be possible for her to use this room for study. He readily agreed and each night she used his desk to work on.

After a while she began to notice the figure of a man nailed to a cross. This fascinated her and she was determined to discover what it meant. As she looked at the figure, she found herself sobbing. On the day of this experience she came to the first of our meetings. My subject was 'The Cross of Christ' and I sought to show something of the love and power of God which was revealed in the death of His Son. She told me after the meeting that she now understood her tears on the previous evening. This was a wonderful illustration of the work of the Holy Spirit. Luke, in his Gospel, records that on one occasion the power of God was present to heal. We found that there were times when the power of God was clearly present and other times when it was less so. At the end of our talks we would invite people forward to the front of the church where we could pray with them. Often this ministry would take up to two hours or more. It meant that many had to stand and queue. One lady told how, whilst waiting to be prayed for, she felt something happening to her infected foot and the side of her left leg which was affected by a skin disease. As she stood there the pain and irritation subsided, and when she looked at her leg and foot she discovered to her amazement that they were perfectly healthy. Another remarkable healing at these meetings was the restoration of sight in a man's damaged eye.

At our final service the cathedral was packed to overflowing. As we began to pray for people literally hundreds flocked forward seeking God's blessing. Bishop Swithian who led the worship came himself and knelt with his clergy asking us to pray for them. Then they prayed for us, before we began ministering together. My most vivid memory of that service was a young man who said he had had a chronic stomach pain over a period of some ten years. As we prayed with him the pain left and he started to laugh. At eleven o'clock when we left he was still sitting in the pew alone laughing and laughing. It appeared as if the Lord was releasing him from a great tension.

In 1984 we spoke at the third national renewal conference at Trivandrum. The following year, Michael Harper being unavailable, I was invited to return to the island and lead a team of twelve for an extended tour. In the summer Bishop Swithian visited London and we met. He was much encouraged by the blessing which had come out of the previous visit and was planning that we should minister in the main cities around the coast where his diocese was. Both of us had a great sense of expectancy and felt that the Lord's hand was upon our meeting and discussion.

Knowing that I was going to be in the area, Bishop Sundar Clark also invited me to be a speaker at the fourth national renewal conference, which was being held in his diocese of Madras. A plan seemed to be emerging for a tour which would involve ministry in Sri Lanka, Madras, and finally Kerala where I had been a number of times before. With Bishop Sundar Clark's invitation to Madras came another from Zacharian Koshy who is a leader in the renewal movement in the Kerala state. However, I have never found

it easy to discern the will of God and at the start of my
travelling ministry I made it a rule never to invite myself to
any situation, however attractive it may have seemed. I
worked on the premise that if God wanted us to send a team
anywhere, then he would commend us to individuals and
churches. Obviously, plans for a visit to India could not be
prepared and carefully tested out with the churches, in the
way they would have been if I had been travelling in the UK
(see chapter 7). At first I felt rather bewildered and was
unsure how to discern whether it was right for us to go.
However, it began to seem that the trip was God's will. In
such circumstances I pray and meditate over the situation. If
during this time I sense a growing peace, then I share it with
Mary. If she feels the same, then I accept.

Then, with only a few weeks before we were to start our
ministry in Sri Lanka, I had an urgent telegram from Bishop
Swithian which simply read: 'Advisable to postpone mission.
Letter follows.' At that time relations between the Tamils
and Singhalese had reached an all-time low. The Singhalese
are predominantly Buddhists and the Tamil minority Hindus. Most of the Christians on the island are Tamils and
converts from Hinduism. Their main Tamil communities are
situated in the north-east of the island where they want to
create an independent homeland.

The original plan had been to begin our northerly ministry
at Jaffna in the North of the island, but this now proved to be
impossible because of the violence and bloodshed. In many
areas of the island curfews were being imposed. Clearly it
was going to be difficult to take a team with me as I had
planned.

Bishop Swithian suggested that I might travel alone to
Colombo and lead a number of renewal meetings based on
various churches in the city. Putting the different invitations
together I decided to fly to Sri Lanka, spend two days
adjusting to the climate, and then fly up to Madras for the
Indian national renewal conference. After Madras I would
go down to Kerala and then have the final ten days in
Colombo.

It is difficult to make the adjustment from a chill English winter to the withering heat of Sri Lanka, and I was glad to be met at the airport by my Tibetan friend, Tenduf-La, and his English wife, Elizabeth. By the time they returned me to the airport to catch the flight for Madras two days later, I was coping with the heat and looking forward immensely to meeting old friends.

At the airport I made my way to the check-in point for the Air Indian flight to Madras. The clerk stamped my ticket and thumbed through my New Zealand passport. He did this a number of times and then said that he was unable to find my visa for entry into India. I told him that on my previous five trips I had never needed a visa and had carefully re-checked this fact both with New Zealand House in London and the Indian High Commission in London. He was adamant – without a visa I couldn't go.

I knew that I was down to give my first talk on the following morning and I had already spent much time in preparation for this. I left the man, and found a seat where I could think and pray about what to do next. As I sat I remembered something which happened to me some years previously. Incredibly I had flown into the United States from Canada and returned without either a passport or a visa. In those circumstances I had been aware of the hand of God. I thought that if the Lord could do that for me in America, he could certainly make a way for me to enter India.

Approaching the Air India check-out point I asked under what conditions they would allow me to fly to Madras. A kindly official told me that if I signed a paper releasing the airline from any responsibility in the case of my deportation, then they would carry me. The flight lasted an hour and during the time I sat and prayed. Arriving at Madras I approached the immigration desk full of faith, excited to see how the Lord would get me into the city. Handing my passport back the official told me he was sorry but he was unable to let me in to India. I asked to see the manager.

It was now late and I sat on my bag and prayed as I waited

for the manager to arrive. He graciously heard my story, sympathised, and then told me that there was no way that I could enter the country and that he would have to deport me. Looking through the partition I could see five pastors who had come from the conference to meet me. The manager allowed us to meet and let me hand over a letter for Bishop Sundar Clark, telling him what had befallen me.

Bewildered, I was marched between two police officers and put back on the aircraft in which I had arrived for the return journey. The next morning I joined a queue of four hundred Indians, Europeans, and others at the Indian High Commission in Colombo to try and get a visa so that I could at least do the Kerala part of the ministry. After three hours in temperatures soaring into the hundreds, I found an official who told me emphatically that the only way I could get a visa for India was to go to my country of origin and apply for one there. He told me it might seem impossible to me, but it was the law to him.

I went home again to my Tibetan friend in a state of shock and uncertainty. Going to my room, I knelt and poured out my heart to God. All I wanted to do now was abort the trip and go home but that hardly seemed right after I had spent so much money on my fare. Many thoughts passed through my mind, including the possibility of bringing the ministry in Colombo forward ten days. Late that evening the thought occurred to me that I should make one last attempt to get into India. So I joined the queue once again and asked to see the highest official available.

The next day I was joined in the queue by two fellow New Zealanders who were hitch-hiking around the world. This was also their last try for a visa and so we decided to work as a threesome. After four hours the manager saw us. By that time I had no more prayers left. I had prayed every way I knew how. I felt that, if I was refused again, then I would go home. We listened with resignation as he went through the rule book and the reasons for the Government's change of immigration policy. He told us that even on that morning he had had a memo reminding him that there were to be no exceptions to the new rule. Suddenly he stood up, took our passports, and disappeared. On his return he told us to fill in a questionnaire – he was going to issue us each with a visa for two weeks.

Sri Lanka and the state of Kerala in southern India are very similar. Kerala, which means 'land of coconuts', is an apt description of the state. The land is laced with streams and lagoons which stock an abundance of fresh-water fish. The staple diet is rice, which is grown in the paddy fields. There are numerous varieties of tropical fruit and at least ten types of banana. According to commonly accepted traditions, St Thomas landed here in AD 52 at the small coastal port not far from Cochin. It was there that he first preached the gospel and today nearly a third of Kerala's 24 million people belong to the Christian community.

I landed in Trivandrum, the capital of Kerala, a day early so there was nobody to meet me. After finding a place to stay, I decided to walk down to the temple area. One of my hobbies is woodwork and on previous visits I had been fascinated to watch the wood carvers, who work near Sri Padmanabhaswamy, the ancient Dravidian temple. I thought it would be a helpful distraction to see them at work again.

Leaving my accommodation I walked towards the temple area through a jungle of people. I passed the fruit sellers and a row of fortune tellers squatting on the pavement, reading the hands of their customers. I stood and watched the carvers for about forty minutes. An old man told me that it took twelve years to learn to carve the intricate Hindu religious figures out of sandalwood.

My spirits were very low as I watched, thinking about the bewildering events of the past few days. I started to stroll back to my room but as I turned on to the main thoroughfare I saw a Westerner carrying a full-size cross, striding at great speed through the crowd. He was some hundred yards from me going in the opposite direction. Much as I felt the need to have someone from the West to talk to, I felt so dejected that initially I could hardly make the effort to follow him. Ten minutes passed and during that time I had a growing inner conviction that I should go and find him.

The heat was still intense as I began to run up the Mahatma Gandhi Road, past the Post Office and towards the Secretariat. This was the main road to the north which I thought was probably the way he had travelled. Getting through the crowds was like arriving late for a Rugby International at Twickenham and trying to push to the front in the north stand area. A number of times I thought I had lost him and almost gave up the chase when suddenly I glimpsed the top of the cross again above the crowd. As I drew level with the walker I could see that he, like me, looked as if he had emerged from the sea fully dressed. We were bathed in perspiration.

The walker with the cross was slightly older and stronger than on that day in 1974 when I had been his host at an Evangelical Alliance conference at Morecambe. That conference had been on evangelism and he had spoken at an impromptu meeting in the dining hall at the end of lunch. He had given an invitation to receive Christ and two or three dozen waiters and waitresses had gone forward – many in tears.

As I walked now beside Arthur Blessitt I introduced myself and reminded him of our Morecambe meeting. I was rather taken aback because he neither looked at me nor did he talk or stop walking. We were approaching the Secretariat building when he eventually stopped, put down his cross, and looked at me. He then proceeded to tell me what had happened to him that day.

Early that morning he had left Cape Comorim with the intention of walking the 600 miles north to Goa. This was his twentieth year of carrying the cross by foot around the world but that morning had been exceptional. As he walked through the villages hundreds, and at times thousands, of people followed after him. At intervals he would stop, put up the cross, and through an interpreter from the region, preach the gospel of Christ. The power of God had been present and dozens had been in tears as they prayed to Jesus for forgiveness and the gift of His Spirit. Many people had been healed and according to Arthur it had been a morning of great joy.

At noon he had rested from the heat till about two, when he had decided to walk on. To his absolute bewilderment nobody followed him or stopped to listen. As he passed by, the people stayed put in the dirty bazaars. Even the children seemed to ignore him, which was most unusual. As he pondered on these things in his mind he sensed the Lord saying that He wanted him in Trivandrum by five o'clock. He took his map out of his shirt pocket and measured the distance. He saw that it was possible only if he walked non-stop for three hours. However, he thought that, if the crowd did gather again, he would preach to them, for this would be a test of whether he was hearing the Lord or not. As he walked he prayed and by four o'clock nobody had gathered and he again felt the Lord saying that He wanted him in Trivandrum by five o'clock in order to meet a man.

As Arthur was telling me this the alarm on his digital watch sounded five 'peeps' and looking straight at me he said, 'You are the man.' At that moment the Holy Spirit came powerfully upon us both and Arthur laid his hands on my head and began to prophesy. The words that he spoke were like shafts of light in a darkened room. He started by saying that the most important thing in my life was not what I did for God, but my own relationship with Him. This was comforting because I felt that somehow I had been letting God down by my failure to get to the Conference at Madras. In a week of travelling all I had done was counsel and pray for an ambassador's daughter and witness to a couple of wealthy English girls on a world tour who had done and seen everything. They had rejected the Catholic faith of their youth and found nothing in Eastern religions and for an hour at Colombo airport they had questioned me about Jesus Christ.

The second part of Arthur's prophecy was that when Jesus opens the door Satan cannot shut it, and if Jesus shuts a door Satan is unable to open it. He told me that though I might not understand what had happened to me God wanted me to know that I was in His will and His blessing was upon me. By this time streams of tears were coursing down my cheeks. We embraced each other and began to worship and praise the Lord. We must have been doing this for fifteen minutes, when we looked up and found that the main road was blocked. There were people as far as the eye could see and police were trying to clear a way for the traffic.

Taking the cross, Arthur moved to higher ground and began to preach the good news of Jesus. Although English is widely known, his interpreter was speaking in Malayan and every so often Arthur would stop and encourage him to shout the gospel message louder. At his prayer of commitment many people showed by the raising of their hands that they wanted to become disciples of Jesus and were consciously calling upon Him.

Before we parted Arthur told me of an experience which, in some way, had been similar to mine. He was once walking with his cross through Borneo when he felt it right to visit a tribe that lived high in the mountains. He had bought some provisions and, in spite of some local reluctance, managed to hire porters to carry them for him. After a search he also found a man who spoke the tribal language of the mountain people. All these factors seemed to confirm a call from the Lord to visit this tribe up in the mountains. It was necessary to take a long hazardous walk through the forest to reach them. All was going well until the beginning of the third day when, in the evening, his helpers became frightened and ran off into the jungle, leaving him completely alone. However, he decided to push on and eventually arrived at a primitive village. The natives crowded out to meet him and were obviously intrigued by this white man carrying a large wooden cross. He was given an area of a hut to sleep in and lay all night quite bewildered by his predicament.

Though he now had no interpreter he decided to try and explain the gospel by acting the parables which Jesus told. The villagers just fell about laughing. Then he tried acting out the crucifixion and the resurrection and this caused both astonishment and amusement. In despair he huddled in his hut and wished he was home with his wife Beryl and the family. It was then that the Lord began to show him that he had been so busy travelling for the Lord that in fact he had had little time to be still and listen. He realised then that the Lord had brought him up to the mountain to take time for meditation and prayer, and so he relaxed and stayed where he was for a week.

After Arthur had left me, I went back to my room to pray and thank the Lord for His incredible kindness to me. There are eight hundred million people in India and the last person I had expected to meet there was Arthur. But the Lord had brought us together here very briefly just to encourage me, and to show me in a fresh and wonderful way that He knew my needs exactly. Arthur had set off on his walk towards Trivandrum for that five o'clock meeting while I was still in the Air Lanka plane over the Gulf of Mannar.

With renewed confidence I caught the train up to Quilon where I stayed with Professor Suman Geevarhghese and her family. Her mother is one of the most wonderful ladies I have met. She is now in her ninety-third year and so full of the Holy Spirit that most of her days and nights are spent in intercessory prayer. She gets up at daybreak, takes her Bible, her stick, and walks through the village looking for people with whom she can share her faith and for whom she can pray. Every day she has a fresh account of what the Lord has done.

On the Sunday I spoke at the Mar Thoma church where Suman was a member. The previous year we had led a series of meetings based on this church and the Lord had blessed many people. This time I spoke on the cross and prayed with a number of people. A young girl was filled with the Holy Spirit and spoke in tongues. I had a 'word of knowledge' about a man with a deep hurt in his heart. This man came for prayer, obviously in severe pain. He said that he had constant pain in all his limbs. As I prayed for his inner hurt he began to weep and in a short time the pain had left his body and hope had come into his life.

Because of the apparent hopelessness in many families, suicide is not uncommon. Often a daughter is married by arrangement to a man who is violent to her. A number who had suffered bereavement through suicides were at this service and I sought to minister the healing of Christ to these broken hearts.

Returning to Suman's home I was asked to pray for a Hindu servant girl. Her neck was apparently stuck in a forward position and she was unable to speak. Suman told me that, a few months before, her husband had found the responsibility of providing for the family too much for him and had taken his life. This widow had been left with two young children, but no home or money. As we prayed the Holy Spirit came upon her and she started sobbing. All at once she began moving her head around. Finally her voice returned and she began to speak.

A characteristic of this trip was the way I saw the Lord working in the hearts of children. I first became conscious of it at a meeting to which Suman took me. This was a special meeting of the leaders of the Christian fellowships whose members worked in the Civil Service. It was held in Kayonkulan, a few hours by train from Quilon, and was held outside under a great awning put up to protect us from the sun.

When the chairman had finished a business agenda I was invited to speak. I spoke of Jesus' love and His knowledge of us all, and illustrated it from my recent experience with Arthur Blessit. At the conclusion the chairman thanked me and immediately introduced another item of business. It seemed that to these leaders the word of God was just an item on an agenda. However, there were a number of children there who began to weep silently as soon as I began to talk about Jesus. Afterwards I prayed for them and the Holy Spirit came upon them powerfully.

Kottayam is further up the coast and it is here that Zachariah and Ramini Koshi live. Zachariah is an ordained minister of the Church of South India and has been involved in the renewal movement since the first conference in Madras where he received the fullness of the Spirit. Zachariah had organised a number of meetings for me. The first one was held in a large room attached to his home. Most of those who came were either converts from Hinduism or practising Hindus from a nearby village.

Some came who were afflicted by evil spirits, which is a not uncommon phenomenon in Indian villages. With Zachariah acting as my interpreter I spoke on the ministry of Jesus to release the captives. At the end of the meeting there were a number of demonic manifestations and many of those troubled in this way were freed in the name of Jesus. The following evening we had double the number, as those touched by Christ the previous evening brought their neighbours and friends. Some believed in Jesus for the first time and others, including a lame girl, received healing from Jesus.

I was so looking forward to returning to Thiruvalla for the convention. It was here three years previously that I had spoken morning and evening for a whole week. A large Panda (a flat roofed tent) had been erected in the extensive church grounds and each evening it had been packed to overflowing with people from the immediate area. During those meetings I spoke on different aspects of the person and work of the Holy Spirit and gave opportunity for people to come for personal prayer. With the help of local church leaders we often prayed for people well into the night.

On these evenings I had many times found myself in tears as in Jesus' name we prayed for the blind, the maimed, and little children with raging fevers. None of those present could ever have afforded proper medical treatment or hospitalisation. We had all sensed a real flow of the warming power of the Holy Spirit during these times and now I was keen to return and learn of the lasting effects of our previous visit.

Pastor Philip and his wife, Susannamanna, welcomed me back to their home. He told me that after the last convention many people had testified to having been healed and fourteen prayer groups had sprung up spontaneously in the area.

These were still meeting and had become a source of renewal for many people.

The convention this time was held in St Thomas' church – a large Victorian structure with wide open windows which, with the fans, made the atmosphere bearable. From the first day the building was packed to overflowing and the Lord ministered powerfully each evening through His Holy Spirit.

Again many children responded to the good news of Jesus. They walked forward and just stood quietly with tears streaming down their little dark cheeks. These children had not been corrupted by television or the expectations of western materialism. Here was an innocence I had rarely encountered before. They weren't perfect, of course, but there was an incredible ability to receive the Holy Spirit who rested upon dozens of them. A number stood sometimes for thirty minutes, lost in their oneness with God.

The gift of miracles was upon the ministry at this time and many people gave testimony to spontaneous healing from physical ailments of one kind or another. I prayed for a lady who, the previous year, had been bitten by a snake. This had resulted in her losing all feeling in her right arm and leg. I started to pray for her, and Pastor Philip, who was translating, told me that she could sense nothing at all happening to her. Instantly I felt the Lord telling me to speak to the poison in her system. Not fully understanding what that might mean, I said, 'In Jesus' name I rebuke the poison in this child of God and command it to go.' Hardly had I spoken these words than her leg and arm started moving. She told Philip that all the feeling was seeping back into her limbs. To God be the glory!

After India it was sobering to return to the tension-filled tropical island of Sri Lanka. Bishop Swithian of Colombo had arranged a programme based on various churches and the cathedral. It was such a privilege to bring the hope of the gospel message into the congregations and to see the Lord confirming what was said by signs and wonders. However, although there was much to encourage, my final memory was a sad one.

On the last evening I had supper with an Assistant Governor of Police in the city, a Tamil and a committed Christian. In the area of the city where they live, there had been serious community riots and gangs had rampaged down their road, breaking up homes and beating Tamil families.

During the meal I sat at the head of the table with my back to the door and facing the family. Before eating we had prayed at some length together and were enjoying each other's company and fellowship when suddenly there was a knock on the door. The children froze as their father went to see who it was. I could not fail to sense that tension and fear; for many Tamils it is difficult to trust the Lord for protection in such circumstances.

Chapter 12

THE MARKET PLACE

For a decade now I have led teams of lay Christians from our church to share their faith with other churches and help in their evangelistic outreach. We find that lay people often communicate the Christian faith better than clergy. They are more readily listened to and less threatening to meet. Many of these church congregations already have small 'home groups' which serve as a basic network for our outreach.

Members of our team visit these groups, to which non-Christian friends have been invited in order to meet us. Usually a lot of prayerful and thoughtful preparation has taken place before our arrival. It is not uncommon for us to lead up to eighty meetings in a week, involving eight hundred people or more gathered into homes to hear and discuss the claims of Christ. During the day our members meet up with the more established groups in the local church.

As I look back over the years, I can see a uniform pattern. After our visits there is usually a deeper work of the Holy Spirit amongst the Christians. Some testify to the healing of relationships and inner hurts. A number experience physical healing and a new freedom in different areas of their lives. However, when it comes to the uncommitted, the picture is not at all encouraging.

Built into all our programmes is a Beginners' Group. This starts on the week after we leave the church, and all who have come to faith or want to know more are encouraged to attend. Usually this numbers between fifteen and thirty. Over 95%

of those who attend will already be on the fringe of the church's life.

It is apparent that much of what we do in our services has little relevance to the outsider. On one Sunday morning I was free of responsibilities and decided to take a friend to hear David Watson. My friend had no experience of traditional religion, and all he knew about Jesus was what I had shared with him.

We travelled some distance and eventually arrived at the church where David was speaking. Within minutes I was seeing what was happening through my friend's eyes. He had never seen a service book, and I had hastily to find the pages for him. The hymns were sung from a collection of four different books whose titles were known only to the initiated.

Later we went for a drink together and discussed what had happened. He liked David Watson and felt that he had communicated to him what it meant to be a Christian. However, he felt quite bewildered by all that had happened. He would never have visited the church by himself, though it was well-known in Christian circles for its renewed life.

David Pytches has a saying that 'the meeting place is the learning place for the market place'. The reason renewed churches are not winning many outsiders to Christ is that we lack confidence in the ability of God to work in the market place. It is not that we haven't faith in the gospel. In the security of our meetings many of us are able to share how Christ is changing our lives and answering prayers.

Since John Wimber's visit to us in 1981 we have begun to discover new ways in which we can share our faith with others. John encouraged us firstly to receive the anointing of the Holy Spirit, and then to learn to minister His presence to others. David Pytches encouraged the church in this and week by week our confidence grew as we experienced God working in our midst.

Peter shared with us a rather humorous experience. Although a young Christian he is involved in the healing ministry at St Andrew's. During the week he works for the BBC as a cameraman. He had called at the office to find his secretary hobbling around on a sprained ankle. Without hesitation, he asked whether she would like him to pray. She greeted his suggestion with much laughter, but then realising he was serious sat down and took off her shoe. Holding her damaged ankle in both hands, he prayed. Suddenly the office door opened and in walked his boss. With raised eyebrows he asked him what he was doing. When Peter replied 'praying for healing' the boss withdrew in embarrassed disbelief. However, later in the day he sought Peter out, as he had noticed how the secretary had been healed. This gave a number of opportunities to talk about Jesus and what he does.

In January/February 1986 a team of ten of us were invited on a six week tour of New Zealand. Our itinerary took us to ten centres and I could see that we would be ministering mainly to Christians. However, in my preparation I felt that there would be opportunities to share the gospel of Christ in the market places. My first opportunity came more quickly than I expected.

We had a stop-over at Singapore where we were looked after by Bonu and Alice at their beautiful Garden Hotel. Coming from an extreme English winter, we quickly made use of the fabulous facilities. After exhausting ourselves in the exercise room we squeezed into the sauna. The heat soon became too intense and the others retreated, leaving me alone. Suddenly the door opened and a young woman came in. We exchanged pleasantries and she started to read a magazine. I sensed that Jesus wanted to work in her life, so I asked her what she did. Her reply was not clear – I thought she said she was a ballet dancer, but it transpired that she was a belly dancer, who had been working in Bangkok and was having a short holiday in Singapore with a boy friend.

Monica then asked me what I was doing. This gave me the opportunity to speak of Jesus. When seeking to draw a person into a discussion about faith I always give them a way of concluding the conversation if they so wish. I therefore asked her whether she knew Jesus, or was seeking Him, or had ever given Him a thought. She replied that she had been thinking about faith because in her words her young sister had 'got involved in religion'. She also said that she had learned about Jesus at Sunday School. I continued to talk about what it meant to know Jesus and she didn't seem to want to go though by this time the cabin had risen to an incredible temperature and perspiration was running off us in streams.

Numerous times I have had similar conversations on church premises and have seen God work. This gave me the confidence to ask Monica if she would like me to pray with her so that she might know Jesus. She replied in the affirmative. In my prayer I invited the Holy Spirit to come and make Jesus known. He immediately came upon her as she asked Jesus into her life. After about ten minutes I asked her what was happening. She opened her eyes and said that she was full of a wonderful peace. Later I encouraged her to read Mark's Gospel, and begin to relate the whole of her life to Jesus simply by talking to Him about it.

Arriving in New Zealand, our team led a conference in Dunedin, and over 1,200 packed the Knox church for a final act of worship. During this meeting I felt that the Lord was telling me that on the following day we should witness in the centre of the city. I invited all who were available to join with us. To my surprise almost a hundred assembled. We walked along Princess Street, praising the Lord to the accompaniment of guitars and tambourines.

The Octagon is the centre of the city. This area comprises a number of spacious lawns surrounded by gardens where the office workers meet to eat their lunches and enjoy the sunshine. On our arrival we formed a semi-circle, and as we worshipped Debbie danced. Soon a crowd gathered, and between songs I spoke about Jesus and what He had come to do.

In the midst of this activity we began to receive words of knowledge. Debbie said that she felt that there was a lady in the crowd who had a lump on her chest. I added further details which the Lord showed me: 'She is in her early thirties, married with two children – a boy and girl. This was diagnosed fourteen days ago and she is feeling fearful.' I repeated this 'word' as loudly as possible. Immediately, from the edge of the crowd, a lady appeared. Half an hour later she was telling me how the lump had disappeared after prayer.

While this was taking place Joan was talking to a young woman. She asked her what she thought of what was being said about Jesus. She replied that she was unable to see that it had any relevance to her. At that moment a word of knowledge was given. John felt that there was a girl in her twenties present who had a sporting injury in her knee and lower thigh. Joan told the young woman what God was saying, and explained that He wanted to heal a girl with that condition. She laughed and replied that it was her. While she was saying how irrelevant God was to her, God was saying how relevant she was to Him!

She agreed to our suggestion that we should pray with her. To her amazement, as soon as the Holy Spirit was invited to come upon her, her leg became numb. This sensation was followed by intense heat, and then tingling throughout the leg. She was a runner and the pain only came after running a mile, so we suggested she run home to test it out. As she ran off she said she would invite Jesus into her life at home, and we directed her to a lively church we knew.

As we travelled north, God continued to give us opportunities outside the church buildings and conference halls. At Christchurch we had a gathering in the square in front of the cathedral. Again we found that worship, dance and drama are instrumental in attracting people, but the vital part comes through private conversations with individuals.

I was asking the Lord whom I should speak with when my attention was drawn to two men in their early twenties. I went over to sit next to them on the steps and asked them what they thought about what was being said. It transpired that they were from Scandinavia, on a world tour which had taken them to New Zealand via India. Their Indian experience had made them think deeply about God, and they were interested to know about my experience of Jesus. After almost an hour one of the men said that he would like to know Jesus and asked me to pray with him. His friend didn't want such prayer, but said that he would pray alone. As we prayed the Holy Spirit came powerfully and poured the life of Jesus into their hearts.

We are learning to minister God's power in the friendly atmosphere of the church, much as the disciples learned in the physical presence of Jesus, but we must never forget that the disciples were later told to go out into all the world. We must accept the same obligation to preach the kingdom and demonstrate its power outside the cosy confines of our church fellowship even if sometimes it seems like having to walk on water. After all that God has shown us of his wonderful power, how can we refuse to take this further step of faith.